A SELF HELP BOOK ABOUT BELIEVING IN YOURSELF A STEP BY STEP GUIDE

TABLE OF CONTENTS

ABOUT THE AUTHOR

Positive B. White is not just a name; it's a mantra for life. A beacon of positivity, a catalyst for change, and an embodiment of unwavering self-belief, Positive B. White has dedicated his life to inspiring others to reach their full potential.

Born and raised in Atlanta, Georgia, Positive B. White's journey was not one of privilege or entitlement. Instead, it was a testament to the power of self-belief, resilience, and hard work. From humble beginnings, he learned the value of perseverance and the art of turning obstacles into stepping stones.

His educational journey led him to the University of West Georgia, where he earned a bachelor's degree in business administration. But his thirst for knowledge didn't stop there. He continued his studies in aviation management at Clayton State University, a testament to his unwavering commitment to growth and self-improvement.

As he grew older, Positive B. White's passion for basketball continued to burn brightly. At the age of fifteen, he earned the coveted title of "Best Offensive Player," a testament to his relentless drive and dedication to his craft. These experiences on the court taught him that success is not merely about talent but also about belief in oneself and the willingness to put in the effort to achieve one's dreams.

Positive B. White's journey wasn't just about personal success; it was about lifting others along the way. He understood the importance of mentorship and guidance in the pursuit of greatness. As an entrepreneur, philanthropist, and motivational speaker, he founded Positive Passionate Motivated Advertising LLC, a platform dedicated to empowering individuals and businesses to realize their full potential.

One of Positive B. White's core beliefs is that self-belief is the cornerstone of success. Throughout his life, he has harnessed the power of self-belief to overcome challenges, set audacious goals, and turn dreams into reality. His journey is a testament to the transformative power of belief in oneself.

As an author, Positive B. White now shares his wealth of knowledge and experience with readers worldwide. This book, a comprehensive guide to self-belief, is a culmination of his life's work—a roadmap for individuals seeking to unlock their full potential and lead lives of purpose and fulfillment.

Positive B. White's mission is clear: to inspire, motivate, and guide individuals on their journey to unwavering self-belief. He believes that everyone possesses the power to shape their destiny, and it all begins with believing in oneself.

Join Positive B. White on this remarkable journey towards self-belief, and discover the incredible heights you can achieve when you choose to believe in yourself.

CHAPTER 1

1.1 THE POWER OF SELF-BELIEF

It was a chilly autumn morning when I realized the profound impact self-belief had on my life. The crisp air seemed to carry a sense of anticipation, mirroring the expectant faces that filled the room. I stood at the front, my heart pounding, about to deliver a presentation that would determine the fate of my fledgling business. Doubt, that ever-present companion of ambitious endeavors, whispered in my ear, reminding me of all the reasons I might fail. But in that pivotal moment, I made a conscious choice—a choice that would alter the trajectory of my life.

- I chose to believe in myself.
- I chose to believe in my abilities.
- I chose to believe in the message I was about to deliver.

In that room, as I gazed out at the audience, something incredible happened. The nervousness that had gripped me, like icy fingers around my heart, began to melt away. It transformed into a powerful surge of confidence that coursed through my veins. The doubts that had clouded my mind, casting shadows of uncertainty, were replaced by a resolute determination to succeed. As I took that first step forward and began to speak, I could feel the energy in the room shift. My words, once hesitant, now flowed with conviction. My gestures, once timid, exuded confidence. And my message, once uncertain, resonated with the audience.

By the time I finished that presentation, I knew I had achieved something extraordinary. It wasn't just the applause or the nods of approval; it was the realization that I had tapped into a wellspring of inner strength—the power of self-belief.

The Transformative Power of Self-Belief

That experience was a turning point in my life, one that taught me a lesson I carry with me to this day: the power of self-belief is unparalleled. It has the potential to shape not only our confidence but also our decisions and, ultimately, our destiny. Self-belief is the compass that guides us through life's turbulent seas, the wind that fills our sails when the waters are rough.

But what exactly is self-belief? It's more than just confidence or self-esteem. It's the unwavering conviction that resides deep within you, whispering, "You have what it takes." It's the unshakable faith that, no matter the obstacles that may arise, you possess the skills, knowledge, and resilience to overcome them and achieve your goals.

Self-belief is the unspoken mantra of champions, the driving force behind audacious dreams, and the beacon that leads us out of the darkest of times.

It's not a fleeting feeling; it's a steadfast belief in your abilities and potential. It's not a hollow affirmation; it's a foundational element of your character.

Understanding the Essence of Self-Belief

Throughout this book, we will delve deep into the concept of self-belief. We will explore its many facets, dissecting it like a multifaceted gem to reveal its brilliance. We will uncover the science behind self-belief, the psychology that underpins it, and the real-world stories that illuminate its path.

We will examine how self-belief is not a one-size-fits-all concept. It takes on different forms and expressions in various aspects of our lives. It influences how we approach our careers, how we nurture our relationships, and how we pursue our passions. It's the silent partner in our decision-making process, often influencing the choices we make without us even realizing it.

The Impact of Self-Belief on Confidence

To truly grasp the power of self-belief, we must first understand its profound impact on our confidence. Confidence, that elusive quality that can make the difference between seizing an opportunity and letting it slip away, is intimately connected to self-belief.

Imagine a tightrope walker high above a bustling city. With each step, the crowd below watches in awe. What allows the tightrope walker to perform such a daring feat with grace and poise? It's not just skill and practice; it's an unwavering belief in their ability to maintain balance and conquer fear. It's self-belief.

Confidence is not the absence of fear; it's the belief that you can face fear head-on and emerge victorious. When you believe in yourself, your confidence soars. You walk a little taller, speak a little clearer, and face challenges with a boldness that commands respect.

In my own journey, I've experienced how self-belief can transform moments of self-doubt into opportunities for growth. I vividly recall the early days of my entrepreneurial venture when every client meeting felt like a high-stakes endeavor. The weight of responsibility bore down on me, and doubts crept in like unwelcome guests. But I had a secret weapon—my unshakable self-belief.

It wasn't arrogance; it was a quiet assurance that I could deliver value, solve problems, and exceed expectations. That self-belief allowed me to navigate those challenging meetings with grace and confidence. It wasn't that I didn't encounter difficulties; it's that I approached them with the unwavering belief that I could find a way through.

The Ripple Effect of Self-Belief

But the impact of self-belief goes beyond personal confidence. It extends to our interactions with others, shaping the way they perceive us and, in turn, how they respond to us. When you believe in yourself, you convey that belief to those around you. Your colleagues, clients, and peers can sense your self-assuredness, and in turn, they are more likely to trust and respect your abilities.

Consider a leader who stands before their team, facing a critical decision. Their words carry the weight of the choice ahead. In that moment, their team looks to them for guidance and assurance. What sets apart a leader who inspires confidence and one who fosters doubt? It's often their self-belief.

When a leader believes in themselves and their vision, their team is more likely to rally behind them. They exude confidence in their decisions, and that confidence becomes contagious. It's not about being infallible; it's about having the conviction to lead with purpose and adapt in the face of uncertainty.

In essence, self-belief is the silent conductor of the orchestra of our interactions. It sets the tone for how others perceive us, and it influences the harmony of our relationships. It's not a magic wand that erases challenges or guarantees success, but it's the unwavering faith that you have what it takes to face those challenges and strive for success.

The Choice of Self-Belief

Self-belief is not a gift reserved for a select few; it's a choice available to each of us. It's a choice to believe in ourselves, to nurture our inner strength, and to cultivate the unwavering conviction that we can overcome obstacles and achieve our goals.

In the chapters that follow, we will delve deeper into the essence of self-belief. We will explore its roots, understand its impact on our outlook on life, and uncover practical strategies to nurture and strengthen it. Self-belief is not a destination; it's a journey—one that begins with the choice to believe in yourself. So, join me as we embark on this transformative journey and unlock the boundless potential of self-belief.

In the next chapter, we will explore the link between self-belief and success, diving into real-life examples of individuals who believed in themselves and achieved remarkable feats. Their stories serve as beacons of inspiration, illuminating the path that self-belief can pave toward personal and professional success.

1.2 THE LINK BETWEEN SELF-BELIEF AND SUCCESS

In the realm of human achievement, few factors wield as much influence as self-belief. It's the intangible force that propels individuals to surmount seemingly insurmountable obstacles, to dream big and chase those dreams relentlessly. In this chapter, we will embark on a journey to explore the profound link between self-belief and success. We will dissect the anatomy of self-belief and how it intertwines with personal and professional triumphs. To illuminate our path, we'll walk alongside real-life heroes who, armed with unwavering self-belief, have conquered their fears and reached the pinnacle of success.

The Foundation of Success: Belief in Oneself

Success, in its myriad forms, is a destination many aspire to reach. Whether it's excelling in a chosen career, achieving financial abundance, nurturing fulfilling relationships, or mastering a skill, success is the culmination of effort, determination, and often, self-belief.

Understanding the Nature of Self-Belief

Self-belief, at its core, is a profound faith in one's abilities and potential. It's the unwavering confidence that you possess the requisite skills and inner strength to surmount obstacles and realize your goals. But it's not merely about puffing up your chest and exclaiming, "I can do it!" It's a deeply rooted, intrinsic conviction that quietly whispers, "I am capable."

The Influence of Self-Belief on Personal Success

Personal success encompasses a wide spectrum of achievements, from personal growth to the pursuit of happiness. It's about becoming the best version of yourself, both in your individual capacities and your contributions to the world. Self-belief is the catalyst that ignites this journey.

Achieving Personal Goals

Whether it's conquering a fear, mastering a new hobby, or striving for physical fitness, personal success often hinges on the belief that you can improve and achieve what you set out to do.

Building Resilience

Life is a series of challenges, and personal success involves weathering these storms with grace and fortitude. Self-belief acts as a shield against self-doubt, enabling you to bounce back from setbacks.

Nurturing Relationships

Confidence in oneself can also positively affect personal relationships. It fosters better communication, assertiveness, and the ability to set healthy boundaries.

From Self-Belief to Professional Triumphs

While personal success is deeply rewarding, professional success often takes center stage in our society. It's the realm of career achievements, financial milestones, and industry recognition. Here, too, self-belief is an indispensable ally.

Believing in Your Career Path

A crucial aspect of professional success is choosing the right career path—one that aligns with your passions, talents, and aspirations. Self-belief plays a pivotal role in this decision-making process.

Identifying Your Passion: Self-belief empowers you to pursue a career that aligns with your passions and interests, as you trust in your ability to excel in your chosen field.

Embracing Challenges: In the professional world, challenges are inevitable. Believing in yourself equips you with the courage to tackle these challenges head-on, viewing them as opportunities for growth rather than insurmountable hurdles.

Maintaining Ambition: Ambition is the driving force behind professional success. Self-belief fuels this ambition, encouraging you to set high goals and work tirelessly to achieve them.

Real-Life Heroes Who Believed in Themselves

To fully appreciate the link between self-belief and success, let's walk alongside some real-life heroes who have harnessed the power of self-belief to accomplish extraordinary feats.

Oprah Winfrey: The Belief That Dreams Are Achievable

Oprah Winfrey, a name synonymous with success and inspiration, emerged from a challenging upbringing to become one of the most influential women in the world. Her journey to success was marked by adversity, but it was her unwavering belief in her ability to make a difference that propelled her forward.

A Traumatic Childhood: Oprah faced poverty, abuse, and adversity during her early years. However, she held onto the belief that her life had a purpose beyond her circumstances.

The Oprah Winfrey Show: Oprah's groundbreaking talk show became a platform for meaningful discussions, touching millions of lives. Her belief in the power of communication and her ability to connect with people fueled her success.

Philanthropy and Impact: Beyond her television career, Oprah has been a passionate philanthropist and advocate for education. Her belief in the transformative power of education has led to the establishment of the Oprah Winfrey Leadership Academy for Girls in South Africa.

Elon Musk: The Belief in the Extraordinary

Elon Musk, the visionary entrepreneur behind companies like SpaceX and Tesla, is known for his audacious goals and unwavering self-belief. His journey from a tech entrepreneur to a space pioneer is a testament to the extraordinary heights one can reach with self-belief.

Founding SpaceX: Musk's belief in humanity's potential to become a multi-planetary species led to the creation of SpaceX, a company with the audacious goal of colonizing Mars.

Electric Revolution: With Tesla, Musk set out to accelerate the world's transition to sustainable energy. His unwavering belief in the electric vehicle's potential has revolutionized the automotive industry.

The Power of Vision: Musk's ability to articulate a compelling vision and his deep-seated belief in the feasibility of his ideas have attracted top talent and significant investments to his ventures.

J.K. Rowling: The Belief in Resilience

J.K. Rowling, the beloved author of the Harry Potter series, faced numerous rejections before her literary success. Her story illustrates the transformative power of self-belief, resilience, and the courage to keep pursuing one's dreams.

Rejections and Challenges: Rowling's initial manuscript for Harry Potter was rejected by multiple publishers. However, her belief in the story's worthiness never wavered.

The Journey to Success: Rowling's journey from struggling writer to best-selling author is a testament to her unwavering belief in her writing abilities and the magical world she had created.

Giving Back: Rowling's success led her to become a philanthropist, believing in the power of education to transform lives. Her establishment of the charity Lumos reflects her commitment to improving the lives of disadvantaged children.

The stories of Oprah Winfrey, Elon Musk, and J.K. Rowling exemplify the undeniable link between self-belief and success. While their paths were diverse, their unwavering confidence in their abilities propelled them to conquer adversity and achieve their dreams.

As we delve deeper into the realms of self-belief and its transformative potential, remember these real-life heroes. Their journeys serve as beacons of inspiration, illuminating the path toward personal and professional success that self-belief can pave. In the following chapters, we will uncover practical strategies to nurture and strengthen this invaluable asset, as well as stories of ordinary individuals who achieved the extraordinary through the power of self-belief.

CHAPTER 2

SETTING CLEAR GOALS

2.1. Defining Your Goals

In the journey of self-belief and personal success, setting clear and achievable goals is akin to charting a course for your ambitions. Goals serve as guiding stars, providing direction and purpose to your efforts. In this chapter, we will delve deep into the significance of setting goals, exploring why they are essential, how they relate to self-belief, and how to identify and define different types of goals—be they career, personal, or otherwise.

The Significance of Setting Clear and Achievable Goals

Imagine embarking on a cross-country road trip without a map or a destination in mind. You might drive aimlessly, but how would you measure progress, let alone reach your intended endpoint? Goals, in the realm of personal development and achievement, are your maps and destinations. They provide clarity, focus, and a sense of purpose to your endeavors.

Why Are Goals Essential?

Clarity

1. Purpose: When you set clear goals, you define your purpose. You know why you're doing what you're doing. This sense of purpose provides a deep and intrinsic motivation to pursue your goals.

2. Focus: Clarity brings focus. With a clear goal in mind, you can direct your energy and attention toward achieving it. You're less likely to be sidetracked by distractions because your vision is well-defined.

3. Eliminating Ambiguity: Ambiguity can be frustrating and lead to indecision. Clear goals eliminate ambiguity by offering a specific target. You know precisely what you're aiming for, reducing confusion.

4. Decision-Making: Setting goals makes decision-making more straightforward. When you're faced with choices, you can assess them against your goals. This makes it easier to determine whether a particular option aligns with your objectives.

5. Confidence: Clarity boosts confidence. Knowing what you want to achieve and having a roadmap to get there instills a sense of purpose and self-assuredness. This confidence can drive you forward, even in challenging times.

Motivation

1. Tangible Target: Goals provide a tangible target to work toward. Instead of vaguely wanting something, you have a specific outcome in mind. This tangibility makes your aspirations more real and achievable.

2. Inspiration: The pursuit of goals can be inspiring. The thought of reaching your objectives, coupled with the anticipation of success, can be a powerful motivator. Goals ignite the fire of determination within you.

3. Persistence: Goals foster persistence. When you encounter obstacles or setbacks, your motivation to achieve your goals can be the driving force that keeps you going. The desire to reach that endpoint fuels your perseverance.

4. Sustained Effort: Clear goals encourage sustained effort over time. They keep you committed to the journey, even when initial enthusiasm wanes. Goals remind you of the long-term rewards.

5. Focus on Rewards: Working toward a goal allows you to focus on the rewards and benefits of achieving it. This focus on the positive outcomes of your efforts can be a potent motivator, driving you to work harder and smarter.

Measurement

1. Tracking Progress: Goals enable you to track your progress. You can measure how far you've come and how much remains to be done. This tracking provides a sense of accomplishment and direction.

2. Objective Assessment: Measurement provides an objective way to assess your achievements. Instead of relying on subjective judgments, you have clear data to evaluate your progress. This objectivity is essential for growth.

3. Feedback Loop: Regular measurement creates a feedback loop. You can adjust your strategies based on data, making your efforts more effective. This continuous improvement is facilitated by the measurement of your goals.

4. Milestone Recognition: Goals often consist of milestones or checkpoints. Achieving these smaller goals along the way provides a sense of accomplishment and motivation. You can celebrate these mini-victories on your journey.

Direction

1. Purposeful Action: With clear goals, your actions become purposeful. You know what you're working toward, and your efforts are intentional. This purposefulness ensures that you're not merely going through the motions but actively pursuing your objectives.

2. Efficiency: Goals make your actions efficient and effective. You don't waste time on activities that don't contribute to your objectives. Your direction ensures that each action serves a purpose.

3. Prioritization: Goals help you prioritize tasks and decisions. You can focus on what matters most and allocate your resources—time, energy, and attention—accordingly. This prevents you from spreading yourself too thin.

4. Consistency: Direction encourages consistency in your actions. You're less likely to be swayed by distractions or unrelated pursuits because your path is clear. This consistency is vital for progress.

Focus

1. Concentration: Clear goals facilitate concentration. When you have a well-defined target, your attention naturally gravitates toward it. This concentration ensures that you're not easily diverted from your path.

2. Eliminating Distractions: Goals help you identify and eliminate distractions that might hinder your progress. You become more discerning about where you invest your time and energy, eliminating activities that don't align with your objectives.

3. Efficient Resource Allocation: Focusing on your goals allows you to allocate your resources efficiently. You prioritize activities and investments that directly contribute to your objectives, optimizing your resource allocation.

4. Avoiding Shiny Object Syndrome: Goals protect you from the "shiny object syndrome," where you constantly chase new ideas or opportunities. Your focus on your goals keeps you grounded and prevents you from being easily swayed by fleeting trends or distractions.

Accountability

1. Commitment: Setting goals represents a commitment to yourself. You've declared your intention to achieve something, and this commitment holds you accountable. You're more likely to follow through on your promises to yourself.

2. Measuring Progress: Goals provide a standard for measuring your progress. You can objectively assess whether you're on track or need to make adjustments. This measurement is a form of self-accountability.

3. Deadlines: Many goals come with deadlines. These deadlines create a sense of urgency and accountability. You're compelled to take action and meet your targets within a specified time frame.

4. Public Declaration: Sharing your goals with others can create external accountability. When people know your objectives, they may check in on your progress, ask about your achievements, or offer support and encouragement. This external accountability can boost your commitment.

Personal Growth

1. Stretching Limits: Ambitious goals encourage you to push beyond your comfort zone. They require you to acquire new skills, adopt new strategies, and explore uncharted territories. This stretching of limits fosters personal growth and development.

2. Learning and Adaptation: Pursuing goals often involves learning new skills and adapting to new situations. These challenges prompt continuous learning and adaptation, contributing to personal development.

3. Resilience: Achieving goals sometimes requires resilience in the face of adversity. Overcoming obstacles and setbacks enhances your resilience and equips you with valuable coping strategies.

4. Confidence Building: As you achieve your goals, your confidence grows. Success breeds self-assuredness, which can benefit all aspects of your life. This confidence is not limited to the specific area of your goals but permeates your entire self-concept.

Incorporating these insights into your understanding of why goals are essential will empower you to set, pursue, and achieve your objectives with greater clarity, motivation, and accountability. It's through this goal-driven journey that you can nurture self-belief and reach new heights in personal and professional success.

The Interplay Between Goals and Self-Belief

Setting and achieving goals are intrinsically tied to self-belief. When you believe in yourself, you are more likely to set ambitious goals. Conversely, as you attain these goals, your self-belief strengthens. This synergy creates a positive feedback loop that propels you toward even greater achievements.

Identifying Different Types of Goals

Goals come in various forms, each serving a unique purpose in your personal and professional life. To harness the power of goal setting effectively, it's essential to recognize these different types of goals and understand how they contribute to your overall success.

Career Advancement

These goals typically revolve around climbing the corporate ladder or reaching higher positions within your field. They represent your aspirations for career growth, increased responsibilities, and the ability to make a more significant impact within your organization.

1. Skill Development: Skill-related goals involve acquiring new competencies, certifications, or expertise. This continuous learning and development can enhance your marketability, job performance, and overall career prospects.

2. Entrepreneurial Pursuits: For aspiring entrepreneurs, these goals involve starting, growing, or managing your own business ventures. They encompass objectives related to business development, market expansion, profitability, and entrepreneurship success.

3. Financial Objectives: Financial goals within a career context often pertain to income, savings, investments, or debt reduction. These goals aim to

improve your financial stability, secure your future, and enable you to enjoy the fruits of your labor.

Personal Development Goals

1. Health and Wellness: Personal development goals in the realm of health and wellness are focused on your physical fitness, nutrition, mental health, and overall well-being. They may involve weight management, regular exercise, meditation, or adopting a healthier lifestyle.

2. Learning and Education: These goals are centered around expanding your knowledge base, pursuing higher education, or developing new talents and skills. Lifelong learning can lead to personal growth, career advancement, and increased self-confidence.

3. Relationships: Personal development also extends to interpersonal relationships. Relationship goals aim to strengthen existing connections, build new relationships, and enhance communication skills. They contribute to emotional intelligence and personal fulfillment.

4. Personal Fulfillment: Personal development isn't solely about career or skills; it also encompasses hobbies, interests, and activities that bring you joy and satisfaction. These goals focus on activities you're passionate about and that contribute to your overall sense of fulfillment.

Financial Goals

1. Savings and Investments: Financial goals related to savings and investments are essential for building wealth and securing your financial future. They involve setting aside money for retirement, emergencies, and other financial milestones. Investing wisely can help your money grow over time.

2. Debt Reduction: If you have loans, credit card debt, or other financial obligations, debt reduction goals are crucial. They provide a structured plan to pay off debts, relieve financial burdens, and achieve a debt-free status.

3. Budgeting and Financial Planning: These goals emphasize creating and adhering to a budget. They also encompass long-term financial planning,

including setting financial milestones, such as buying a home, funding your children's education, or retiring comfortably.

Relationship Goals

1. Family and Parenting: Relationship goals within the family context aim to strengthen bonds and create a harmonious family environment. They may involve spending quality time together, resolving conflicts, or supporting each other's growth.

2. Romantic Relationships: In romantic partnerships, relationship goals often focus on enhancing communication, trust, and intimacy. They seek to build a strong foundation for a healthy, loving relationship or address specific issues.

3. Friendships: Goals related to friendships concentrate on nurturing and deepening your friendships. Whether it's maintaining regular contact, supporting your friends' endeavors, or resolving conflicts, these goals contribute to meaningful and lasting friendships.

Lifestyle and Well-being Goals

1. Travel: Travel-related goals encompass your desire to explore new places, cultures, and experiences. They encourage you to broaden your horizons, create memories, and find inspiration through travel.

2. Work-Life Balance: Achieving work-life balance is a common lifestyle goal. It involves finding equilibrium between your professional and personal life to reduce stress, improve mental health, and enhance overall well-being.

3. Hobbies and Interests: Goals associated with hobbies and interests center on pursuing activities that bring you joy, satisfaction, and a sense of purpose outside of work. They contribute to a balanced and fulfilling life.

Understanding the different types of goals allows you to tailor your goal-setting process to your specific needs and desires. It's essential to strike a balance between these goal categories to lead a fulfilling and well-rounded life.

Setting the Stage for Goal Achievement

Setting clear and achievable goals is the first step in your journey toward success and self-belief. However, merely articulating your goals isn't enough; you must establish a roadmap to reach them. In the following sections of this chapter, we will explore practical strategies to define, refine, and pursue your goals effectively. Additionally, we will delve into the psychology of goal setting and discuss the science behind why goal setting works, providing you with actionable insights to propel your self-belief and achievements to new heights.

2.2: Staying Motivated

Strategies for Staying Motivated Throughout Your Goal-Setting Journey

Motivation is the fuel that propels us forward on our journey towards achieving our goals. It's that inner drive that keeps us focused, persistent, and determined, even when faced with challenges and setbacks. In this chapter, we will explore the intricacies of motivation and provide you with a comprehensive toolkit of strategies to stay motivated throughout your goal-setting journey.

The Dynamics of Motivation

Motivation is a complex psychological state influenced by a variety of factors. Understanding its dynamics can help you harness it effectively.

Intrinsic vs. Extrinsic Motivation

Motivation can be broadly categorized into two types: intrinsic and extrinsic.

Intrinsic Motivation: This form of motivation comes from within. It's driven by personal enjoyment, a sense of accomplishment, or the inherent satisfaction derived from the task itself. Intrinsic motivation is often associated with long-term commitment and a deeper sense of fulfillment.

Extrinsic Motivation: Extrinsic motivation, on the other hand, is driven by external rewards or consequences. It includes factors like money, recognition, or fear of punishment. While extrinsic motivation can be effective in the short term, it may not sustain long-term commitment or passion.

Understanding which type of motivation aligns with your goals and values is crucial. Ideally, your goals should be intrinsically motivating, as they are more likely to inspire lasting dedication.

The Motivation-Habit Loop

Motivation is closely tied to habits. Developing positive habits can boost motivation, making it easier to work towards your goals consistently.

Cue: Triggering Motivation

A cue is what triggers your motivation. It could be an inspiring quote, a personal reminder of your goals, or even the sight of your work desk. Identifying effective cues that resonate with you is an essential step in staying motivated.

Routine: Cultivating Motivation

The routine represents the actions you take to cultivate and maintain motivation. This might involve reading motivational books, practicing visualization, or engaging in activities that boost your mood and energy.

Reward: Reinforcing Motivation

Finally, the reward is what reinforces your motivation loop. It's the sense of accomplishment and satisfaction you experience when you make progress toward your goals. Celebrating small wins along the way can reinforce motivation and keep you moving forward.

Strategies for Staying Motivated

Now that we've explored the foundation of motivation, let's dive into practical strategies to keep your motivation engine running smoothly.

1. Set Clear and Meaningful Goals

The first step in staying motivated is having goals that resonate with your values and aspirations. Clear, well-defined goals provide a sense of purpose and direction. When you understand why you're pursuing a particular goal and how it aligns with your values, you're more likely to stay motivated.

Action Steps:

Define Your "Why": Take time to reflect on why your goal is essential to you. How will it improve your life or the lives of others? The clearer your "why," the stronger your motivation.

Break Down Your Goals: Large, daunting goals can be overwhelming. Break them down into smaller, achievable steps. Each completed step can serve as a mini-victory that boosts motivation.

2. Create a Vision Board

A vision board is a powerful visualization tool. It's a collage of images, quotes, and reminders of your goals and dreams. By regularly viewing your vision board, you reinforce your commitment to your aspirations.

Action Steps:

Gather Visual Inspiration: Collect images, quotes, and symbols that represent your goals and desires. These can be from magazines, the internet, or your personal photographs.

Design Your Vision Board: Arrange your chosen elements on a board or digital platform. Ensure that your vision board is visually appealing and inspiring.

Review Daily: Set aside time each day to review your vision board. Let it serve as a constant reminder of your aspirations.

3. Cultivate a Growth Mindset

A growth mindset is the belief that your abilities and intelligence can be developed through effort and learning. Embracing this mindset can boost motivation because it encourages you to view challenges as opportunities for growth.

Action Steps:

Challenge Negative Self-Talk: Pay attention to your inner dialogue. Replace self-limiting beliefs with statements that reflect a growth mindset. For example, replace "I can't do this" with "I haven't learned this yet."

View Setbacks as Learning Experiences: Instead of seeing failures as defeats, view them as valuable lessons. Ask yourself, "What can I learn from this experience, and how can it make me better?"

4. Maintain a Positive Environment

Your physical and social environment can significantly impact your motivation. Surrounding yourself with positivity can help you stay motivated and focused.

Action Steps:

Declutter Your Space: A cluttered environment can lead to distractions and decreased motivation. Organize your workspace to create a conducive atmosphere for productivity.

Seek Supportive Relationships: Surround yourself with individuals who believe in your goals and provide encouragement. Share your aspirations with supportive friends or join groups with similar interests.

5. Practice Self-Compassion

Self-compassion involves treating yourself with kindness, especially in moments of self-doubt or failure. It's a crucial component of maintaining motivation, as it helps you bounce back from setbacks.

Action Steps:

Practice Self-Kindness: Treat yourself as you would treat a friend. When you make mistakes or face challenges, offer yourself words of encouragement and support.

Avoid Perfectionism: Recognize that perfection is an unattainable standard. Focus on progress rather than perfection, and understand that setbacks are a natural part of any journey.

6. Develop a Routine

A daily routine can provide structure and discipline, making it easier to stay motivated. It helps you build momentum and consistency in your efforts.

Action Steps:

Create a Daily Schedule: Plan your day with specific time slots for goal-related activities. A well-structured routine minimizes procrastination and ensures that you allocate time to work on your goals.

Start with Small Habits: If you're trying to establish a new routine, start with small, manageable habits. Gradually increase their complexity as they become ingrained in your daily life.

7. Track Your Progress

Regularly monitoring your progress helps maintain motivation by providing evidence of your achievements. It also allows you to adjust your strategies if you're not making the progress you desire.

Action Steps:

Use a Goal Journal: Keep a journal dedicated to your goals. Record your daily progress, setbacks, and insights. Reviewing this journal can highlight your journey's successes and areas for improvement.

Celebrate Milestones: Acknowledge and celebrate your achievements, no matter how small they may seem. Recognizing your progress reinforces motivation and builds a sense of accomplishment.

8. Visualize Your Success

Visualization is a powerful technique used by many successful individuals. It involves vividly imagining your success, which can help manifest your goals and maintain motivation.

Action Steps:

Create a Mental Movie: Take time each day to visualize yourself achieving your goals. Imagine the details, emotions, and sensations associated with your success. This mental rehearsal can boost your motivation.

Use Affirmations: Incorporate positive affirmations related to your goals into your daily routine. Repeating these affirmations can reinforce your belief in your ability to achieve your objectives.

9. Stay Adaptable

Maintaining motivation often involves adapting to changing circumstances and overcoming obstacles. Flexibility and resilience are key components of long-term motivation.

Action Steps:

Anticipate Challenges: Identify potential challenges or obstacles that may arise on your journey. Develop strategies for addressing them in advance to prevent motivation dips.

Learn from Setbacks: When you encounter setbacks or obstacles, view them as opportunities to learn and grow. Use your setbacks as stepping stones rather than stumbling blocks.

Overcoming Common Obstacles and Setbacks

Maintaining motivation isn't always smooth sailing. It's essential to anticipate and address common obstacles and setbacks that may threaten your enthusiasm along the way.

1. Procrastination

Procrastination is a common motivation killer. It often stems from fear of failure, perfectionism, or feeling overwhelmed.

Overcoming Procrastination:

Break Tasks into Smaller Steps: Divide your goals into smaller, more manageable tasks. This makes them less intimidating and more achievable.

Set Specific Deadlines: Assign deadlines to your tasks to create a sense of urgency. Use tools like calendars or task management apps to stay organized.

Visualize the End Result: Imagine the sense of accomplishment and satisfaction you'll experience once you complete the task. This visualization can motivate you to start.

2. Self-Doubt

Self-doubt can erode motivation and self-confidence. It often arises when you encounter challenges or face moments of uncertainty.

Overcoming Self-Doubt:

Challenge Negative Thoughts: Identify and challenge self-doubting thoughts. Ask yourself for evidence supporting or refuting these thoughts.

Seek Support and Feedback: Share your concerns with a trusted friend, mentor, or coach. Their feedback and encouragement can help boost your confidence.

Remember Past Achievements: Reflect on your past successes and accomplishments. Remind yourself of your capabilities and resilience.

3. Burnout

Burnout occurs when you push yourself too hard, leading to mental and physical exhaustion. It can sap your motivation and hinder your progress.

Overcoming Burnout:

Prioritize Self-Care: Schedule regular breaks, exercise, and relaxation into your routine. Taking care of your well-being is crucial for maintaining motivation.

Reevaluate Your Goals: If burnout persists, reconsider your goals and their alignment with your values. Adjust or modify them if necessary to reduce the pressure.

Delegate or Seek Help: Don't hesitate to delegate tasks or seek assistance when needed. You don't have to tackle everything on your own.

4. Loss of Interest

Sometimes, you may lose interest in pursuing a particular goal. This can happen if your goals no longer align with your passions or if you've outgrown them.

Overcoming Loss of Interest:

Reconnect with Your "Why": Revisit the reasons you initially set the goal. If it no longer resonates with you, consider if there's a more compelling goal to pursue.

Explore New Avenues: If you've lost interest in a specific goal, explore new interests and passions. Sometimes, pursuing something entirely different can reignite motivation.

Adjust Your Goals: Modify or refine your goals to make them more appealing and aligned with your current desires.

Maintaining motivation is an ongoing journey, much like working towards your goals. By understanding the dynamics of motivation and implementing these strategies, you can cultivate a lasting source of inspiration that propels you toward your aspirations. Remember that motivation may ebb and flow, but with dedication and the right tools, you can keep it burning brightly on your path to success.

CHAPTER 3

OVERCOMING SELF-DOUBT

3.1. Recognizing Self-Doubt

Understanding the Signs and Triggers of Self-Doubt

Self-doubt is a common human experience, a shadow that often creeps in when we least expect it. It's that nagging voice in our heads that questions our abilities, judgments, and worth. In this chapter, we will delve into the intricate world of self-doubt, learning to recognize its signs, uncovering its triggers, and ultimately understanding how to overcome it.

The Nature of Self-Doubt

Before we can conquer self-doubt, it's essential to understand its nature. Self-doubt isn't a monolithic entity; it can take various forms and manifest differently in individuals. However, certain commonalities underpin this universal struggle.

1. Negative Self-Talk

Negative self-talk is a hallmark of self-doubt. It involves a constant stream of self-criticism, where your inner voice berates you with doubts and insecurities. Phrases like "I'm not good enough," "I'll never succeed," or "I don't deserve this" become familiar refrains.

2. Fear of Failure

Self-doubt often accompanies a paralyzing fear of failure. You hesitate to take risks or step outside your comfort zone because you worry about what might happen if you don't succeed. This fear can prevent you from pursuing your goals and dreams.

3. Comparisons to Others

Self-doubt thrives when you constantly compare yourself to others. Whether it's your colleagues, friends, or acquaintances, measuring your success against theirs can lead to feelings of inadequacy and self-doubt.

4. Perfectionism

Perfectionism and self-doubt often go hand in hand. The relentless pursuit of flawlessness creates unattainable standards, making you doubt your abilities whenever you fall short, even slightly.

5. Impostor Syndrome

Impostor syndrome is a specific form of self-doubt where you feel like a fraud, believing that your achievements are merely due to luck or external factors. You fear that one day, you'll be exposed as an impostor.

6. Self-Criticism

Self-doubt fuels self-criticism, which can be harsh and unrelenting. You hold yourself to impossibly high standards, and when you don't meet them, you criticize yourself mercilessly.

The Impact of Self-Doubt

Self-doubt isn't a benign presence; it exerts a profound impact on various aspects of our lives.

1. Decision-Making

Self-doubt can paralyze decision-making. You second-guess every choice, fearing that you'll make the wrong one. This indecisiveness can lead to missed opportunities and increased stress.

2. Confidence Erosion

Continual self-doubt erodes your self-confidence. It creates a negative feedback loop where the less confident you feel, the more self-doubt you experience. This can affect your relationships, career, and overall well-being.

3. Goal Pursuit

Self-doubt can be a significant roadblock on your journey toward your goals. It makes you question whether you're capable of achieving them, leading to procrastination and avoidance.

4. Mental Health

Persistent self-doubt can have detrimental effects on your mental health. It can contribute to anxiety, depression, and low self-esteem, impacting your quality of life.

5. Physical Health

The stress and anxiety resulting from self-doubt can also affect your physical health. It can manifest as sleep disturbances, increased susceptibility to illness, and even chronic health conditions.

The Self-Doubt Triggers

Now that we've explored the nature and impact of self-doubt, it's crucial to recognize the triggers that often give rise to this unwelcome guest.

1. Past Failures

Past failures can be potent triggers for self-doubt. When you've experienced setbacks or disappointments, it's natural to question your abilities and fear a repeat performance.

2. Rejection and Criticism

Rejection or criticism, whether in personal relationships or professional settings, can trigger self-doubt. Negative feedback can reinforce the belief that you're not good enough or that others see your flaws.

3. Comparison to Others

As mentioned earlier, constantly comparing yourself to others can be a significant trigger for self-doubt. When you perceive that others are outperforming you, it can undermine your self-esteem.

4. Perceived Inadequacy

If you believe you lack certain skills, knowledge, or qualifications required for success, this perceived inadequacy can fuel self-doubt. You question whether you're prepared or capable enough to achieve your goals.

5. Fear of Repeating Mistakes

The fear of making the same mistakes again can trigger self-doubt, especially if you've experienced significant consequences from previous errors. This fear can hinder your willingness to take risks.

6. Unrealistic Expectations

Setting unrealistic expectations for yourself can set the stage for self-doubt. When you fall short of these lofty standards, it reinforces feelings of inadequacy.

Overcoming Self-Doubt

Now that we've explored the landscape of self-doubt, let's turn our attention to strategies for overcoming it. Recognizing and acknowledging self-doubt is the first step toward liberation.

1. Self-Awareness

Self-awareness is the cornerstone of overcoming self-doubt. Recognize when self-doubt begins to surface. Pay attention to the negative self-talk, the fear of failure, and the comparisons to others. By identifying these signs, you can address self-doubt more effectively.

Action Steps:

Keep a Journal: Maintain a journal where you record instances of self-doubt. Describe the situations, thoughts, and emotions surrounding it. This helps you spot patterns.

Mindfulness Practice: Engage in mindfulness or meditation exercises to become more attuned to your thoughts and emotions. Mindfulness can help you detach from self-doubt's grip.

2. Challenge Negative Self-Talk

Negative self-talk is a significant contributor to self-doubt. Challenge these inner critics by replacing self-critical thoughts with more balanced and compassionate ones.

Action Steps:

Identify Negative Beliefs: When self-doubt arises, identify the negative beliefs underpinning it. For example, if you think, "I'll never succeed," challenge it with evidence of your past achievements.

Affirmations: Develop positive affirmations that counteract self-doubt. For instance, "I am capable, and I have the skills to tackle this challenge."

3. Embrace Failure as Learning

Instead of fearing failure, reframe it as a valuable learning experience. Understand that setbacks are a natural part of any journey, and they can offer valuable insights and growth opportunities.

Action Steps:

Shift Your Perspective: When you encounter failure, ask yourself what you've learned from the experience. What can you do differently next time?

Celebrate Small Wins: Celebrate your achievements, no matter how minor they may seem. Recognizing your progress can boost your self-esteem and counteract self-doubt.

4. Seek Support

Don't battle self-doubt alone. Reach out to trusted friends, family members, mentors, or a therapist who can provide encouragement and perspective.

Action Steps:

Talk About It: Share your self-doubts and fears with someone you trust. Often, voicing your concerns diminishes their power.

Seek Professional Help: If self-doubt is significantly impacting your life and mental health, consider consulting a mental health professional for guidance and support.

5. Set Realistic Goals

Unrealistic goals can be breeding grounds for self-doubt. Set achievable and realistic objectives that align with your current abilities and resources.

Action Steps:

Break Down Goals: Divide larger goals into smaller, manageable steps. This makes them less overwhelming and more attainable.

Track Progress: Monitor your progress toward your goals. Seeing your accomplishments can boost your confidence.

6. Cultivate Self-Compassion

Practice self-compassion by treating yourself with the same kindness and understanding you'd offer a friend facing similar doubts and challenges.

Action Steps:

Practice Self-Kindness: Treat yourself with gentleness and compassion, especially when you make mistakes or face setbacks.

Self-Encouragement: Offer words of encouragement to yourself as you would to a friend. Remind yourself that self-doubt is a shared human experience.

Self-doubt is a formidable adversary, but it's not invincible. By recognizing its signs, understanding its triggers, and implementing strategies to overcome it, you can regain control over your confidence and decision-making. Remember that self-doubt is a shared human experience, and you have the power to conquer it. In the next chapter, we will explore practical techniques for silencing your inner critic and incorporating positive affirmations into your daily life.

3.2. Strategies for Overcoming Self-Doubt

Practical Techniques for Silencing Your Inner Critic

In the journey to overcome self-doubt, one of the most formidable adversaries you'll face is your own inner critic. This persistent voice inside your head can sow the seeds of doubt, making you question your abilities and worth. However, it's essential to recognize that you have the power to silence this inner critic and replace its negative narrative with one of self-compassion and confidence. In this chapter, we will explore practical techniques and exercises to help you quiet the inner critic that fuels self-doubt.

The Inner Critic: Friend or Foe?

Before we delve into the strategies for silencing your inner critic, it's important to understand its origins and purpose. The inner critic isn't inherently malevolent; it often emerges from a well-intentioned place. It might have developed as a protective mechanism during your formative years, aiming to keep you safe from perceived threats, criticism, or rejection.

However, as you mature, this inner critic can become overly harsh and critical, hindering your growth and self-belief. The key is not to eliminate it entirely but to transform it into a more constructive and supportive voice.

1. Self-Reflective Journaling

Self-reflective journaling is a powerful tool for gaining insight into your inner critic's patterns and triggers. It allows you to step back and objectively observe your thoughts and feelings.

Action Steps:

Set Aside Time: Dedicate a specific time each day or week for journaling. Find a quiet and comfortable space.

Identify Self-Criticism: When self-doubt arises, jot down the critical thoughts you experience. Be as specific as possible.

Question Your Thoughts: Review your critical thoughts and ask yourself if they are based on facts or assumptions. Challenge their validity.

Offer Self-Compassion: Counteract self-criticism with self-compassion. Write down compassionate and encouraging statements to yourself.

Track Progress: Over time, review your journal entries to track your progress in managing and transforming your inner critic.

2. The Power of Mindfulness

Mindfulness is the practice of being fully present in the moment, observing your thoughts without judgment. It can be a potent tool for silencing the inner critic by creating a mental space between you and your self-doubt.

Action Steps:

Mindful Breathing: Take a few minutes each day to focus on your breath. When self-doubt arises, return to your breath to regain composure.

Thought Observation: Practice observing your thoughts without judgment. When self-criticism emerges, view it as a passing cloud in the sky of your mind.

Body Scan: Conduct regular body scans to identify physical sensations associated with self-doubt. Awareness of these sensations can help you manage them.

Gratitude Practice: Counteract self-doubt by acknowledging the positive aspects of your life. Practicing gratitude can shift your focus away from negativity.

3. Cognitive Restructuring

Cognitive restructuring involves identifying and challenging negative thought patterns, replacing them with more balanced and realistic beliefs.

Action Steps:

Identify Negative Thoughts: When self-doubt surfaces, pinpoint the negative thoughts contributing to it.

Question Assumptions: Ask yourself whether these thoughts are based on evidence or assumptions. Are they logical and fair?

Generate Counter-Thoughts: Develop counter-thoughts that challenge the negative ones. For instance, if you think, "I'm not good enough," replace it with, "I have the skills and potential to succeed."

Practice Affirmations: Incorporate positive affirmations into your daily routine. These are brief, powerful statements that reinforce your self-belief.

4. Self-Compassion Practices

Self-compassion involves treating yourself with the same kindness and understanding you'd offer a friend facing similar challenges. It's a potent antidote to self-doubt.

Action Steps:

Self-Compassionate Language: Pay attention to your self-talk. Replace self-criticism with self-compassionate language. Instead of saying, "I'm such a failure," say, "I made a mistake, but I'm learning and growing."

Letter of Self-Compassion: Write a letter to yourself as if you were offering support and encouragement to a dear friend. Express your understanding and kindness.

Mindful Self-Compassion: Engage in mindful self-compassion exercises, where you actively acknowledge and soothe your emotional pain with self-kindness.

5. Visualization and Positive Imagery

Visualization involves mentally picturing a positive outcome or scenario. Using this technique can help silence the inner critic by providing your mind with positive imagery to counteract self-doubt.

Action Steps:

Visualization Routine: Dedicate time each day to visualization exercises. Sit in a quiet space and imagine yourself confidently achieving your goals.

Incorporate Senses: Engage all your senses in the visualization. Feel the emotions associated with success, hear the sounds, and see the vivid details.

Create a Vision Board: Make a physical or digital vision board with images, quotes, and representations of your goals and aspirations. Review it daily for inspiration.

6. Incorporating Positive Affirmations into Your Daily Life

Positive affirmations are concise, affirmative statements aimed at bolstering self-belief and countering self-doubt. They are powerful tools for rewiring your inner dialogue.

Action Steps:

Identify Target Areas: Determine specific areas of self-doubt or insecurity you want to address with affirmations. For instance, if you doubt your abilities at work, create affirmations related to your competence.

Develop Affirmations: Craft positive affirmations that directly address your target areas. Ensure they are concise, present tense, and positively framed. For example, "I am confident in my abilities."

Repeat Daily: Integrate affirmations into your daily routine. Repeat them multiple times a day, such as in the morning, before significant tasks, or when self-doubt arises.

Visual Aids: Create visual aids, such as sticky notes or digital reminders, displaying your affirmations. Place them where you'll frequently see them.

Silencing your inner critic is a journey that requires patience and consistent effort. The strategies discussed in this chapter—self-reflective journaling, mindfulness, cognitive restructuring, self-compassion practices, visualization, and positive affirmations—are powerful tools at your disposal. Remember that transforming your inner critic is not about erasing self-doubt entirely but about shifting the balance toward self-compassion, self-belief, and resilience. In the next chapter, we will explore the concept of embracing failure as a stepping stone and delve into practical strategies for learning and growing from setbacks.

CHAPTER 4

EMBRACING FAILURE AS A STEPPING STONE

4.1. Reframing Failure

Viewing Failure as a Learning Opportunity

Failure—a word that often carries a heavy weight, laden with negative connotations. It's a word that many of us have been conditioned to fear and avoid at all costs. However, in the journey of self-belief, it's crucial to reevaluate our relationship with failure. Instead of seeing it as an endpoint, we must learn to view it as a vital stepping stone on the path to success.

In this chapter, we will explore the concept of reframing failure. We'll delve into the profound shift that occurs when you begin to see failure not as an outcome to dread but as a classroom for growth. We'll examine why failure is a natural part of any meaningful endeavor and how, by embracing it, you can extract valuable lessons and experiences that propel you forward.

The Nature of Failure

Before we can truly embrace failure as a stepping stone, it's essential to understand its nature. Failure is not a verdict on your worth or abilities. It is not a dead-end or a reflection of your potential. Failure is, in fact, a common companion on the journey to success. It's a teacher, a mentor, and a catalyst for growth.

1. Failure as Feedback

Imagine you're embarking on a cross-country road trip. As you drive, you occasionally encounter road signs indicating detours, obstacles, or caution ahead. You don't interpret these signs as personal failures; they are merely feedback guiding your journey. Similarly, failures are like road signs on your path to success. They provide feedback, indicating where adjustments or detours are necessary.

2. Failure as a Teacher

Consider some of history's greatest innovators, such as Thomas Edison or Steve Jobs. They didn't view their countless setbacks as failures; they saw them as lessons. Edison famously said, "I have not failed. I've just found 10,000 ways that won't work." Failure, in this sense, is a powerful teacher, illuminating the pathways to improvement and innovation.

3. Failure as Growth

Every time you encounter failure and persevere, you grow stronger and more resilient. It's akin to a muscle that becomes more robust with each challenge. By reframing failure as a growth opportunity, you can turn setbacks into stepping stones toward personal and professional development.

Personal Stories of Turning Setbacks into Success

To illustrate the transformative power of reframing failure, let's explore the stories of individuals who faced significant setbacks yet emerged stronger, wiser, and more determined.

1. Walt Disney: The Rejected Cartoonist

Walt Disney is a name synonymous with creativity and imagination. Yet, before he became an iconic figure in animation, he faced a series of failures and rejections. His first animation company, Laugh-O-Gram Studio, went bankrupt. He was fired from a job at a newspaper because he lacked creativity. And, to add to the list, his first creation of a character, Oswald the Lucky Rabbit, was stolen by his distributor.

What sets Walt Disney apart is not the absence of failures but his ability to reframe them as opportunities. When Oswald was taken from him, Disney didn't give up. Instead, he channeled his setback into creating something new—Mickey Mouse. This beloved character became the foundation of an empire that redefined entertainment.

2. J.K. Rowling: From Rejection to Wizardry

J.K. Rowling, the author of the immensely popular Harry Potter series, faced numerous rejections before her work found a publisher. She was a struggling single mother dealing with poverty and depression. Yet, her resilience and belief in her story led her to persevere.

Rowling's journey from failure to success demonstrates the power of tenacity and the willingness to learn from setbacks. She transformed her life, not by avoiding failure, but by using it as a source of motivation and creativity.

3. Michael Jordan: The Basketball Legend

Michael Jordan, widely regarded as one of the greatest basketball players of all time, encountered failure on his path to greatness. In his early career, he faced a significant setback when he was cut from his high school basketball team. This rejection could have discouraged him, but Jordan used it as fuel to improve his skills and determination.

Jordan's story teaches us that failure, even in the pursuit of our passions, can serve as a catalyst for self-belief and growth. His relentless work ethic and commitment to self-improvement are a testament to the idea that setbacks are not roadblocks but opportunities to become exceptional.

Strategies for Reframing Failure

Now that we've explored the transformative potential of reframing failure, let's delve into practical strategies for implementing this mindset shift in your life.

1. Cultivate a Growth Mindset

Psychologist Carol Dweck introduced the concept of a growth mindset, which emphasizes the belief that abilities and intelligence can be developed through dedication and hard work. Embracing a growth mindset allows you to view failure as a natural part of the learning process. It encourages resilience and a focus on improvement rather than avoidance of failure.

Action Steps:

Practice Self-Compassion: Treat yourself with kindness and understanding when you encounter setbacks. Avoid self-criticism and recognize that everyone faces failures.

Use "Not Yet": Instead of saying, "I can't do this," say, "I can't do this yet." This subtle shift in language reinforces the idea that your abilities are evolving.

Set Learning Goals: Focus on goals that involve acquiring new skills or knowledge rather than just achieving outcomes. This places the emphasis on the process of growth.

2. Analyze and Learn

When you face failure, it's essential to engage in a constructive analysis of what went wrong. This analytical approach shifts your perspective from dwelling on failure to extracting valuable lessons.

Action Steps:

Debrief After Failures: Take time to reflect on what led to the failure. Was it a lack of preparation, a specific mistake, or external factors beyond your control?

Identify Patterns: Look for recurring patterns in your failures. Are there specific areas where you tend to stumble? Identifying patterns can help you proactively address them.

Extract Lessons: Ask yourself what you've learned from the experience. How can you apply these lessons to future endeavors? Every failure carries insights that can be invaluable.

3. Embrace Resilience

Resilience is your ability to bounce back from adversity. It's a crucial trait for reframing failure. Resilient individuals view setbacks as challenges to overcome rather than insurmountable obstacles.

Action Steps:

Build Resilience Skills: Practice techniques such as mindfulness, stress management, and emotional regulation to enhance your resilience.

Seek Support: Reach out to friends, mentors, or support groups during challenging times. Sharing your experiences can provide emotional support and new perspectives.

Maintain Perspective: Keep in mind that one failure does not define your entire journey. Maintaining a long-term perspective can help you see setbacks as temporary.

Reframing failure is a transformative shift in perspective that empowers you to view setbacks as opportunities for growth and learning. By recognizing that failure is not the opposite of success but an integral part of it, you can navigate your self-belief journey with resilience, determination, and an unwavering commitment to personal and professional development.

In the next chapter, we will explore the importance of surrounding yourself with positivity, cultivating a supportive network, and filtering out negativity to further nurture your self-belief.

4.2: Learning and Growing

In the previous section, we explored the concept of reframing failure and how it can be a stepping stone to success. Now, we will delve deeper into the critical aspect of learning and growing from these experiences. Failure is not the end; it's an opportunity for growth, a chance to refine your skills, and a pathway to bolster your self-belief.

This chapter will provide you with valuable strategies for learning from your failures and setbacks. We will also uncover the profound connection between resilience and building self-belief. Resilience isn't merely about bouncing back; it's about using adversity as a catalyst for personal and professional development.

Strategies for Learning from Failures and Setbacks

1. Reflect with Purpose

Reflection is the cornerstone of learning from failure. It's not merely about replaying events in your mind but conducting a purposeful analysis. When reflecting on a setback, consider these steps:

Identify the Factors: Determine the factors that contributed to the failure. Was it a lack of preparation, external circumstances, or a specific mistake?

Recognize Patterns: Are there recurring patterns in your failures? Identifying these patterns allows you to proactively address them in future endeavors.

Extract Key Insights: What have you learned from this experience? Each failure carries valuable insights that can be applied to future challenges.

2. Embrace a Growth Mindset

A growth mindset is the belief that abilities and intelligence can be developed through dedication and hard work. This mindset is crucial for learning from failures because it shifts your perspective from avoiding failure to embracing it as a pathway to growth.

Practice Self-Compassion: Be kind to yourself when you encounter setbacks. Avoid self-criticism, and remind yourself that failure is a part of the journey for everyone.

Use "Not Yet": Change your language from "I can't do this" to "I can't do this yet." This subtle shift reinforces the idea that your abilities are evolving.

Set Learning Goals: Instead of solely focusing on outcomes, emphasize goals that involve acquiring new skills or knowledge. This shift places importance on the process of growth.

3. Seek Constructive Feedback

Feedback is a powerful tool for growth. Seek feedback from mentors, peers, or supervisors regarding your failures. Constructive feedback provides an external perspective that can help you gain insights into areas for improvement.

Be Open to Feedback: Embrace feedback, even if it's critical. Constructive criticism is an opportunity to identify areas that require growth.

Act on Feedback: Don't simply collect feedback; take actionable steps to address the areas highlighted for improvement.

4. Develop a Growth Plan

After a setback, create a growth plan that outlines your strategies for improvement. This plan should be specific, measurable, and time-bound. It acts as a roadmap for your journey from failure to success.

Set Clear Goals: Define precise goals related to the areas that need improvement. These goals provide direction and focus.

Establish Milestones: Break down your goals into smaller milestones. Achieving these milestones provides a sense of accomplishment and progress.

Monitor Progress: Regularly assess your progress toward your goals. Adjust your strategies as needed.

5. Leverage Failure as Motivation

Failure can be a potent source of motivation. Instead of letting it deter you, channel the energy from your setbacks into renewed determination.

Setbacks as Fuel: Use your failures as motivation to prove to yourself that you can overcome challenges. Turn the frustration or disappointment into determination.

Visualize Success: Create a vivid mental image of your success, especially in the areas where you've faced setbacks. Visualization can be a powerful motivator.

The Role of Resilience in Building Self-Belief

Now that we've explored strategies for learning from failures and setbacks, it's essential to understand how resilience plays a vital role in the process of building self-belief.

What is Resilience?

Resilience is the ability to bounce back from adversity, adapt to challenges, and endure difficult situations. It's not about avoiding failures but about facing them with strength and determination.

The Interplay Between Resilience and Self-Belief

Resilience and self-belief are interconnected in a profound way:

Resilience Enhances Self-Belief: When you're resilient, setbacks don't shatter your belief in yourself. Instead, they strengthen it. Resilience allows you to view failures as temporary roadblocks, not as insurmountable obstacles.

Self-Belief Fuels Resilience: Conversely, self-belief is a foundation for resilience. When you genuinely believe in your abilities and potential, you're more likely to bounce back from adversity. You see challenges as opportunities to prove your capabilities.

Building Resilience

Resilience is not a fixed trait; it can be cultivated and strengthened over time. Here are strategies to enhance your resilience:

Practice Mindfulness: Mindfulness techniques can help you stay grounded and calm during challenging times. They enable you to approach setbacks with a clear mind.

Build a Support System: Lean on your friends, mentors, and support groups during difficult moments. Sharing your experiences and seeking guidance can boost your resilience.

Maintain Perspective: Keep a long-term view of your journey. Remember that one setback does not define your entire trajectory. This perspective helps you weather the storms.

Learn from Role Models: Study individuals who have displayed resilience in the face of adversity. Their stories can provide inspiration and insights into building your resilience.

Learning and growing from failures and setbacks is an integral part of the self-belief journey. Failure is not a destination but a path to growth, a chance to refine your skills, and a means to bolster your self-belief. By embracing a growth mindset, seeking constructive feedback, and channeling failure into motivation, you can turn setbacks into stepping stones on your path to success.

CHAPTER 5

BUILDING A SUPPORTIVE NETWORK

5.1. The Importance of Supportive Friends, Mentors, and Allies

In the journey to strengthen self-belief and achieve your goals, the company you keep plays a pivotal role. The people around you, including friends, mentors, and allies, have a profound impact on your mindset, outlook, and ability to overcome challenges. This chapter explores the significance of cultivating a supportive network and provides insights into how to identify and nurture positive relationships.

The Power of Your Network

Before we delve into the specifics of building a supportive network, it's crucial to understand why this network is vital in your quest to enhance self-belief.

1. Emotional Resonance

Positive relationships offer emotional support. During challenging times, having friends or mentors who understand, empathize, and encourage you can make a world of difference. Their emotional resonance can help you stay motivated and resilient.

2. Diverse Perspectives

A network composed of diverse individuals brings diverse perspectives. These perspectives can open your mind to new ideas, strategies, and approaches to challenges. They prevent you from being trapped in a single worldview.

3. Accountability

A supportive network holds you accountable for your goals and commitments. When others know about your aspirations, you're more likely to stay on track and take action.

4. Inspiration and Motivation

Surrounding yourself with positive and ambitious individuals can be highly motivating. Their success stories and determination can inspire you to aim higher and believe in your potential.

Identifying Supportive Relationships

Now that we understand the importance of a supportive network, let's discuss how to identify such relationships.

1. Trust and Respect

Supportive relationships are built on trust and mutual respect. You should feel safe sharing your aspirations, challenges, and vulnerabilities with these individuals. They should respect your goals and provide constructive feedback.

2. Positive Influence

Positive relationships influence you positively. These individuals should uplift and encourage you rather than drag you down. They should share your enthusiasm for your goals and believe in your abilities.

3. Availability and Accessibility

Supportive friends, mentors, or allies are available when you need them. They are willing to lend an ear, offer advice, or provide assistance when you face obstacles.

4. Shared Values

Shared values are the foundation of enduring relationships. While differences in opinions can be enriching, a core set of shared values ensures alignment in the long run.

5. Constructive Feedback

A supportive network doesn't merely offer praise; it also provides constructive feedback. They are honest with you, pointing out areas where you can improve while offering encouragement.

Cultivating Positive Relationships

Building a supportive network is an ongoing process that requires effort and intentionality. Here are strategies to cultivate positive relationships:

1. Networking Events

Attend networking events, seminars, or workshops related to your interests and goals. These gatherings are fertile grounds for meeting like-minded individuals who share your passions.

2. Online Communities

Join online communities, forums, or social media groups focused on your areas of interest. Engage in discussions, seek advice, and connect with individuals who resonate with your goals.

3. Seek Mentors

Mentors play a pivotal role in personal and professional growth. Identify individuals who have achieved what you aspire to accomplish. Reach out to them, express your admiration, and ask for guidance.

4. Reciprocity

Supportive relationships are a two-way street. Be willing to offer your support, advice, or assistance to others as well. Reciprocity fosters trust and strengthens connections.

5. Regular Communication

Consistent communication is essential for maintaining relationships. Check in with your network regularly, share updates about your goals, and show genuine interest in their endeavors.

6. Quality over Quantity

It's not about the quantity of connections but the quality. Focus on nurturing a few meaningful relationships rather than collecting a large number of superficial ones.

The Impact of a Supportive Network on Self-Belief

Your network can significantly influence your self-belief in several ways:

1. Validation

Supportive individuals validate your aspirations and beliefs. When they express faith in your abilities, it bolsters your self-belief.

2. Encouragement

Supportive friends and mentors provide encouragement during challenging times. Their words of encouragement remind you that you're not alone on your journey.

3. Accountability

Knowing that others believe in your goals makes you more accountable. You're more likely to take consistent action when you have an audience that expects your progress.

4. Resilience

Supportive relationships provide emotional cushioning during setbacks. They remind you that failures are temporary, and you have the strength to overcome them.

5. Inspiration

Witnessing the achievements of your network members can be highly inspiring. It shows you that success is attainable and within reach.

Building a supportive network of friends, mentors, and allies is a significant step in your journey to enhance self-belief. These relationships offer emotional support, diverse perspectives, accountability, and inspiration. By identifying and cultivating positive relationships, you create a nurturing environment that fosters self-belief.

In the next section, we will explore the importance of filtering out negativity from your life, understanding its detrimental impact, and implementing strategies to maintain a positive and constructive mindset.

5.2: Filtering Out Negativity

Strategies for Minimizing Exposure to Negative Influences

In the pursuit of self-belief and personal growth, one of the most critical steps is to filter out negativity from your life. Negativity can take many forms, including pessimism, criticism, self-doubt, and toxic relationships. These influences can erode your confidence, hinder your progress, and drain your enthusiasm. This chapter explores strategies for recognizing and minimizing exposure to negative influences while creating a nurturing and positive environment conducive to your growth.

The Impact of Negativity

Before we delve into the strategies to filter out negativity, it's crucial to understand why this step is essential for building and maintaining self-belief.

1. Undermining Self-Belief

Negative influences can erode your self-belief. Constant exposure to criticism or pessimism can make you doubt your abilities and potential.

2. Reducing Motivation

Negativity saps your motivation and enthusiasm. It can make your goals seem unattainable and drain your energy to pursue them.

3. Stifling Growth

To grow and thrive, you need a nurturing environment. Negativity stifles personal growth and can keep you stuck in unproductive patterns.

4. Impairing Decision-Making

Negative influences can cloud your judgment. They can lead to self-doubt and indecision, hindering your ability to make confident choices.

Identifying Negative Influences

Recognizing negativity is the first step in filtering it out. Negative influences can come from various sources, including people, media, and even your own thoughts.

1. Negative People

Identify individuals in your life who tend to be critical, pessimistic, or unsupportive. These individuals may include friends, family members, coworkers, or acquaintances.

2. Media and Information

Evaluate the media and information sources you expose yourself to regularly. Some news, social media, or entertainment can be overwhelmingly negative.

3. Self-Criticism

Pay attention to your inner dialogue. Self-criticism and self-doubt can be powerful negative influences.

4. Comparison

Constantly comparing yourself to others can lead to feelings of inadequacy and negativity.

Strategies for Minimizing Exposure to Negativity

Once you've identified negative influences, it's time to implement strategies to minimize your exposure to them.

1. Set Boundaries

Establish clear boundaries with individuals who bring negativity into your life. Politely but firmly communicate your limits and let them know that you prefer positive interactions.

2. Choose Your Media Wisely

Be selective about the media you consume. Opt for sources that provide valuable information without unnecessary negativity. Limit your exposure to sensationalized or distressing news.

3. Practice Mindfulness

Mindfulness techniques can help you become more aware of negative thoughts and emotions as they arise. This awareness allows you to address them and choose a more positive perspective.

4. Positive Affirmations

Use positive affirmations to counteract self-criticism and self-doubt. Regularly remind yourself of your strengths, capabilities, and past achievements.

5. Surround Yourself with Positivity

Prioritize spending time with people who uplift and encourage you. Cultivate relationships with individuals who share your goals and values.

6. Limit Negative Conversations

When engaging in conversations, steer clear of topics that tend to turn negative. Instead, focus on subjects that inspire and motivate you.

7. Practice Gratitude

Gratitude can shift your focus from what's lacking to what's abundant in your life. Regularly practice gratitude to foster a positive mindset.

8. Self-Care

Invest in self-care practices that promote well-being and reduce stress. Activities like exercise, meditation, and hobbies can help you stay positive.

Creating a Nurturing and Positive Environment

Filtering out negativity isn't just about removing negative influences; it's also about actively creating a nurturing and positive environment.

1. Surround Yourself with Positivity

Fill your life with positive influences. This includes spending time with supportive individuals, reading uplifting books, and watching inspiring content.

2. Set Goals and Intentions

Setting clear goals and intentions gives you a sense of purpose and direction. It provides a positive focus for your efforts.

3. Continuous Learning

Engage in continuous learning and personal development. The pursuit of knowledge and skills can be highly motivating and positive.

4. Visualization

Practice visualization to maintain a positive outlook. Visualize your goals and success regularly to reinforce your self-belief.

5. Celebrate Achievements

Acknowledge and celebrate your achievements, no matter how small. Celebrations can boost your confidence and maintain a positive mindset.

6. Help Others

Contributing to the well-being of others can be profoundly positive. Volunteer or support causes that resonate with you.

The Impact of a Positive Environment on Self-Belief

A nurturing and positive environment has a profound impact on your self-belief:

1. Boosted Confidence

Positivity reinforces your self-confidence. It reminds you of your capabilities and potential.

2. Enhanced Motivation

A positive environment fuels your motivation. It makes your goals seem attainable and exciting.

3. Fostered Growth

Positivity encourages personal growth. It inspires you to overcome challenges and embrace new opportunities.

4. Clearer Decision-Making

A positive mindset enhances your decision-making abilities. It helps you approach choices with confidence.

5. Resilience

Positivity cultivates resilience. It equips you to bounce back from setbacks with unwavering self-belief.

Filtering out negativity from your life and creating a nurturing and positive environment are essential steps in your journey to strengthen self-belief. By recognizing and minimizing exposure to negative influences, you protect your confidence and motivation. Simultaneously, actively fostering positivity in your environment ensures that you remain inspired, focused, and determined to achieve your goals.

CHAPTER 6

THE POWER OF VISUALIZATION

6.1. The Role of Visualization

Visualization, often referred to as mental imagery or guided imagery, is a powerful tool that can profoundly impact your self-belief and contribute to your overall success. It involves using your imagination to create detailed mental images of your desired outcomes, goals, and aspirations. In this chapter, we will delve into the significance of visualization, exploring how it can shape your self-belief and discussing various forms of visualization techniques.

The Essence of Visualization

Visualization is not merely daydreaming or wishful thinking; it is a deliberate mental practice that involves engaging your senses to create a vivid mental picture of your goals. When you visualize, you are essentially rehearsing success in your mind before it becomes a reality. This process has the power to influence your subconscious mind, making your aspirations feel more attainable and real.

How Visualization Impacts Self-Belief

1. Enhanced Confidence

Visualization fosters a sense of confidence and self-assuredness. When you repeatedly see yourself succeeding in your mind's eye, it erases doubt and reinforces your belief in your abilities.

2. Positive Self-Talk

Through visualization, you can replace negative self-talk with positive affirmations. It allows you to shift from thoughts like "I can't do it" to "I am capable and confident."

3. Emotional Regulation

Visualization helps you manage emotions associated with self-doubt or fear of failure. It enables you to visualize yourself remaining calm and composed, even in challenging situations.

4. Goal Clarity

Visualization enhances goal clarity. When you have a clear mental image of your goals, it becomes easier to set specific, achievable objectives.

5. Improved Focus

Visualizing your goals regularly sharpens your focus. It reminds you of what truly matters, reducing distractions and enhancing productivity.

Forms of Visualization Techniques

Visualization techniques vary in complexity and style, but they all share the common goal of harnessing the power of imagination to enhance self-belief. Let's explore some of the most effective forms of visualization:

1. Guided Visualization

Guided visualization involves listening to a recorded script or guide that directs your imagination. The guide helps you create a mental image of your desired outcome step by step. These scripts often incorporate sensory details to make the experience more vivid.

2. Mental Rehearsal

Mental rehearsal is a visualization technique used by athletes, performers, and professionals to prepare for future events. It involves mentally practicing a skill or task, envisioning each step in detail. This form of visualization is particularly effective for building confidence in specific abilities.

3. Vision Boards

A vision board is a physical representation of your goals and aspirations. It typically consists of a collage of images, words, and symbols that reflect your desired outcomes. By creating and regularly viewing a vision board, you reinforce your self-belief and keep your goals at the forefront of your mind.

4. Creative Visualization

Creative visualization is a flexible technique that allows you to construct and manipulate mental images that resonate with you personally. You can use it to visualize anything, from career success to personal growth. It encourages creativity and a deep connection with your goals.

5. Positive Affirmations with Visualization

Combining positive affirmations with visualization is a potent technique. While repeating affirmations, you simultaneously create mental images that align with those affirmations. For example, if your affirmation is "I am confident," you visualize yourself confidently achieving your goals.

6. Scripting Your Ideal Day

Scripting involves writing a detailed account of your ideal day as if it has already happened. This written visualization exercise can help you clarify your goals and feelings associated with success.

Developing Your Visualization Practice

To harness the full potential of visualization and enhance your self-belief, follow these steps to develop your visualization practice:

1. Set Clear Goals

Before you can visualize your success, you need to define your goals clearly. The more precise your goals, the more effective your visualization will be.

2. Find a Quiet Space

Choose a quiet, comfortable space where you can relax without distractions. Visualization is most effective when you are at ease.

3. Practice Regularly

Consistency is key. Dedicate time each day to practice visualization, preferably in the morning or before significant tasks.

4. Use All Your Senses

Incorporate sensory details into your visualizations. Imagine not just what you see but also what you hear, smell, taste, and feel.

5. Stay Positive

Maintain a positive and optimistic mindset during your visualization sessions. Focus on your achievements, not your doubts or fears.

6. Embrace Emotions

Allow yourself to feel the emotions associated with success during visualization. Whether it's joy, confidence, or pride, experiencing these emotions reinforces your belief in yourself.

7. Stay Patient

Visualization is a skill that develops over time. Be patient with yourself and trust the process.

Incorporating visualization into your daily routine can be a transformative practice. As you refine your ability to create vivid mental images of your goals, you'll find that your self-belief strengthens, and success becomes an even more attainable reality.

6.2. Step-by-Step Guide to Creating a Vision Board

Creating a vision board is a dynamic and creative visualization exercise that serves as a tangible representation of your goals, dreams, and aspirations. It's a powerful tool that reinforces your self-belief and keeps your objectives at the forefront of your mind. In this section, we'll provide a comprehensive, step-by-step guide on how to create your vision board effectively.

The Essence of a Vision Board

A vision board, often referred to as a dream board, is a collage of images, words, and symbols that represent your goals and desires. It serves as a visual reminder of what you want to achieve in various aspects of your life, from career and personal growth to health and relationships. The act of creating a vision board helps you clarify your goals and reinforce your self-belief.

Materials You'll Need

Before you embark on creating your vision board, gather the following materials:

A Poster Board or Canvas: This will serve as the base for your vision board. You can choose a size that suits your preferences, but a larger board provides more space for creativity.

Magazines and Images: Collect magazines, newspapers, or printouts of images and words that resonate with your goals. These will be the building blocks of your vision board.

Scissors: You'll need scissors to cut out images and words from magazines.

Glue or Double-Sided Tape: To adhere the images and words to your board.

Markers, Pens, or Stickers: These can be used to write or embellish your vision board.

Ruler: It can help you ensure that your images are straight and aligned.

Step-by-Step Guide

Now, let's dive into the process of creating your vision board:

Step 1: Set Clear Intentions

Before you start, take some time to reflect on your goals. What do you want to achieve in your career, personal life, relationships, health, and other areas? It's crucial to have a clear understanding of your aspirations.

Step 2: Gather Your Materials

Collect all the materials you'll need, as mentioned above. Ensure you have a diverse selection of magazines and images that cover various aspects of your life.

Step 3: Create a Quiet Space

Find a quiet and comfortable space where you can work on your vision board without distractions. Consider playing calming music or lighting a candle to set a peaceful atmosphere.

Step 4: Visualization and Selection

Begin by visualizing your goals. Imagine yourself already achieving them and the emotions associated with that success. As you do this, start flipping through the magazines and images, selecting ones that resonate with your vision.

Step 5: Cut and Organize

With your scissors, carefully cut out the selected images and words. Sort them into categories based on the areas of your life they represent. For example, have one pile for career-related images and another for personal growth.

Step 6: Arrange and Glue

Start arranging the images and words on your poster board or canvas. There's no specific rule for placement; go with what feels right to you. You can create separate sections for different life areas or arrange them in a more freeform style.

Step 7: Add Personal Touch

Use markers, pens, or stickers to add personal notes, quotes, or affirmations to your vision board. These can further reinforce your self-belief and add a personalized touch to your board.

Step 8: Review and Reflect

Once your vision board is complete, take a step back and look at it as a whole. Reflect on the images and words you've chosen and the emotions they evoke. Visualize yourself living the life you've depicted on your board.

Step 9: Display Your Vision Board

Place your vision board in a location where you'll see it daily. This could be in your bedroom, office, or any space where you spend a significant amount of time. The key is to keep it visible.

Step 10: Regularly Engage

Your vision board is not a one-time creation. Engage with it regularly. Spend a few minutes each day visualizing your goals and reflecting on the images and words on your board. As you make progress toward your objectives, you can add new images or update existing ones.

Incorporating Daily Visualization Practices

Creating a vision board is just one facet of daily visualization practices. To further enhance your self-belief and manifest your goals, consider incorporating these daily habits:

1. Morning Visualization Routine

Start your day with a short visualization session. Close your eyes, take a few deep breaths, and visualize yourself achieving your daily goals with confidence and success. Feel the emotions associated with your accomplishments.

2. Gratitude Journaling

Maintain a gratitude journal where you jot down things you're thankful for daily. This practice shifts your focus toward positivity and reinforces your belief in the abundance of life.

3. Affirmations

Incorporate positive affirmations into your daily routine. Choose affirmations that align with your goals and repeat them regularly. For example, if your goal is career-oriented, you might say, "I am confident and capable in my career."

4. Visualization Meditation

Engage in guided visualization meditation sessions. These often involve a narrator leading you through a mental journey toward your goals. It's a powerful way to reinforce your self-belief.

5. Evening Reflection

Before bed, take a few moments to reflect on your day. Visualize the successes you've achieved, no matter how small. This practice encourages a positive mindset and reinforces your belief in your abilities.

Creating a vision board and incorporating daily visualization practices into your routine can significantly enhance your self-belief and accelerate your journey toward your goals. These practices serve as constant reminders of your aspirations and keep your self-belief strong, even in challenging times.

Remember that self-belief is not about empty optimism; it's about developing a profound confidence in your capabilities. Your vision board and daily visualization rituals will serve as powerful tools on your path to self-belief and success. Embrace them fully, and watch as they transform your life

CHAPTER 7

TAKING ACTION

7.1. From Belief to Action

In the preceding chapters, we've explored the incredible power of self-belief and the various strategies to nurture and strengthen it. Now, it's time to bridge the gap between belief and realization, between dreams and actual achievements. This is where the rubber meets the road in your self-belief journey. In Chapter 7, we'll discuss why taking action is a crucial step, how it aligns with your self-belief, and how to overcome the obstacles that often stand in the way.

The Paralysis of Inaction

Before delving into the importance of taking action, let's address a common challenge many individuals face: the paralysis of inaction. This occurs when self-doubt, fear, or procrastination prevents you from translating your self-belief into concrete steps toward your goals. You might have unwavering belief in your capabilities, but without action, it remains a mere potential waiting to be unlocked.

Belief and Action: A Symbiotic Relationship

Your self-belief and actions are intricately connected, forming a symbiotic relationship. Here's how they influence each other:

1. Belief Drives Action: Self-belief serves as the driving force behind your actions. When you genuinely believe in your abilities, you're more likely to take on challenges, pursue opportunities, and persevere in the face of setbacks.

2. Action Reinforces Belief: Conversely, taking action reinforces your self-belief. When you set goals and work toward them, you accumulate evidence of your capabilities and achievements. This, in turn, bolsters your self-belief.

3. Inaction Fuels Self-Doubt: On the flip side, prolonged inaction can erode your self-belief. When you consistently hesitate or avoid taking necessary steps, self-doubt can creep in, causing you to question your abilities.

Overcoming Procrastination

Procrastination is a common obstacle to taking action. It's the tendency to delay or avoid tasks, especially those that require effort or stepping out of your comfort zone. Here are strategies to overcome procrastination and unleash your self-belief:

1. Set Clear Goals: Break your larger goals into smaller, manageable tasks. This not only makes them less overwhelming but also provides a clear roadmap for action.

2. Prioritize Tasks: Identify the most crucial tasks and tackle them first. This ensures that you're making progress on your top priorities.

3. Use the Two-Minute Rule: If a task can be completed in two minutes or less, do it immediately. This simple rule prevents the accumulation of small, easy-to-complete tasks that can contribute to procrastination.

4. Create a Routine: Establishing a daily or weekly routine can help you build consistency in your actions. When tasks become habitual, they're less likely to be postponed.

5. Visualize Success: Spend a few moments visualizing the positive outcomes of taking action. This can motivate you to overcome procrastination.

6. Accountability: Share your goals with a trusted friend, mentor, or coach who can hold you accountable. Knowing that someone is monitoring your progress can be a powerful motivator.

7. Use Time Management Techniques: Explore time management methods like the Pomodoro Technique, time blocking, or Eisenhower's Urgent/Important Principle to boost productivity.

8. Address Perfectionism: Perfectionism often leads to procrastination, as the fear of not doing something perfectly can be paralyzing. Embrace the concept of "good enough" and focus on progress rather than perfection.

9. Silence Your Inner Critic: The inner critic can feed procrastination by highlighting self-doubt. Practice self-compassion and challenge negative self-talk.

Overcoming Self-Limiting Behaviors

Self-limiting behaviors are actions or habits that hinder your progress and limit your potential. Recognizing and addressing these behaviors is essential for translating self-belief into positive actions. Here are common self-limiting behaviors and how to overcome them:

1. Self-Sabotage

Self-sabotage often occurs when you undermine your own efforts or success. It can manifest as procrastination, negative self-talk, or fear of success. To overcome self-sabotage, seek professional help if needed and practice self-awareness to identify triggers.

2. Fear of Failure

The fear of failure can paralyze you and prevent you from taking necessary risks. To conquer this fear, reframe failure as a learning opportunity. Embrace a growth mindset that views challenges as a path to improvement.

3. Negative Self-Talk

Negative self-talk can undermine your self-belief and discourage action. Challenge these negative thoughts by replacing them with positive affirmations and realistic self-assessments.

4. Comfort Zone Stagnation

Staying within your comfort zone can lead to stagnation and missed opportunities. Push yourself to step outside of your comfort zone regularly. Start with small challenges and gradually expand your boundaries.

5. Comparison Trap

Constantly comparing yourself to others can diminish your self-belief and deter action. Focus on your journey and progress rather than external benchmarks.

6. Lack of Self-Confidence

Low self-confidence can hinder your willingness to take action. Boost your self-confidence by setting achievable goals, practicing self-compassion, and acknowledging your accomplishments.

7. Perfectionism

Perfectionism can stall progress as you strive for unattainable standards. Embrace imperfection and focus on continuous improvement rather than flawless outcomes.

The Power of Small Steps

Taking action doesn't always require giant leaps. In fact, significant progress is often the result of consistent small steps. Don't underestimate the impact of incremental actions. They build momentum, reinforce self-belief, and bring you closer to your goals.

From belief to action—this transition is where the magic happens. Your self-belief serves as the driving force, and action is the vehicle that propels you toward your aspirations. In this chapter, we've explored the symbiotic relationship between self-belief and action, as well as strategies to overcome procrastination and self-limiting behaviors.

Remember that self-belief is not a passive state; it's a dynamic force that thrives on action. By taking deliberate steps toward your goals, you not only validate your self-belief but also manifest your potential. In the following chapters, we'll delve deeper into staying accountable, celebrating your wins, and cultivating resilience—essential elements of your self-belief journey.

7.2. Staying Accountable

Strategies for Staying on Track and Being Accountable to Your Goals

In the journey of turning self-belief into action, accountability is your compass. It guides you, keeps you on track, and ensures that your belief in yourself translates into tangible results. Accountability is not just a system of checks and balances; it's a conscious choice you make to take ownership of your goals. In this chapter, we will explore the strategies for staying accountable to your goals and understand the significance of consistency and perseverance.

The Role of Accountability

Before we delve into the strategies, let's examine why accountability is a critical component of success. Accountability serves multiple essential functions in your self-belief journey:

1. Keeps You Focused: When you're accountable to your goals, you stay focused on your priorities. It prevents distractions and keeps you from straying off course.

2. Provides Structure: Accountability introduces structure into your goal-setting process. It breaks down your goals into actionable steps and sets deadlines.

3. Measures Progress: Being accountable allows you to measure your progress objectively. It provides clear indicators of what's working and what needs adjustment.

4. Motivates Action: Knowing that you are accountable to someone or something motivates action. It ignites a sense of responsibility and encourages you to follow through.

5. Builds Resilience: Accountability helps you build resilience. When you encounter setbacks, having a system of accountability ensures you get back on track rather than giving up.

Strategies for Staying Accountable

Now, let's explore practical strategies to stay accountable to your goals:

1. Set SMART Goals: Ensure your goals are Specific, Measurable, Achievable, Relevant, and Time-bound (SMART). This clarity makes it easier to track progress.

2. Create a Goal Timeline: Develop a timeline that outlines milestones and deadlines for your goals. Having a visual representation of your journey keeps you accountable to your timeline.

3. Accountability Partners: Consider having an accountability partner, such as a friend, mentor, or coach. Share your goals with them, and schedule regular check-ins to discuss your progress.

4. Use Technology: Utilize apps, tools, or software designed for goal tracking and accountability. These can help you monitor your progress, set reminders, and visualize your achievements.

5. Journaling: Maintain a journal or diary to record your daily or weekly progress. Reflect on your accomplishments, setbacks, and lessons learned.

6. Public Declaration: Sometimes, publicly declaring your goals can be a powerful motivator. Share your aspirations on social media, a blog, or with a community that aligns with your interests.

7. Reward System: Establish a reward system tied to your goals. Celebrate your achievements, no matter how small, as a form of positive reinforcement.

8. Visual Aids: Create visual aids, such as vision boards or progress charts, that display your goals and milestones. Visual reminders can help you stay committed.

9. Regular Review: Set aside time for regular goal reviews. Assess your progress, adjust your strategies if needed, and reaffirm your commitment.

10. Accountability Groups: Join or form an accountability group with like-minded individuals pursuing similar goals. Group dynamics can provide encouragement and support.

11. Consequences: Establish consequences for not meeting your commitments. While this approach may not work for everyone, it can be effective for some individuals.

12. Professional Coaching: Consider working with a professional coach who specializes in goal achievement and accountability. Coaches provide guidance and hold you responsible for your actions.

13. Document Your Journey: Whether through blogs, vlogs, or personal documentation, sharing your journey with others can be a form of external accountability.

The Importance of Consistency and Perseverance

Accountability is not a one-time effort but a continuous process that requires consistency and perseverance. Here's why these qualities are crucial:

1. Consistency: Consistency is the key to building habits that support your goals. When you consistently take action, it becomes a part of your routine and requires less effort over time.

2. Perseverance: Challenges and setbacks are inevitable on any journey. Perseverance is your ability to push through difficulties, adapt to changes, and stay committed to your goals despite obstacles.

Overcoming Accountability Challenges

While accountability is vital, it's not without its challenges. Here are some common obstacles and how to overcome them:

1. Fear of Failure: The fear of not meeting your commitments can be paralyzing. Embrace the mindset that failures are learning opportunities, not indicators of your worth.

2. Lack of Motivation: Motivation can wane, but discipline remains constant. Even on days when motivation is low, rely on your commitment and discipline to stay accountable.

3. Overcommitment: Avoid overloading yourself with too many goals and commitments. Quality is more important than quantity. Focus on a few meaningful goals.

4. Neglecting Self-Care: Don't sacrifice self-care for the sake of accountability. Prioritize your physical and mental well-being, as they directly impact your ability to stay accountable.

5. Resistance to Feedback: Be open to feedback, even if it's critical. Constructive feedback can help you course-correct and improve your accountability strategies.

Staying accountable to your goals is not just a strategy; it's a mindset. It's a commitment to your aspirations, a recognition of your potential, and a promise to yourself. In this chapter, we've explored why accountability is crucial, practical strategies to implement it, and the importance of consistency and perseverance.

As you continue your journey, remember that accountability is your ally, not your adversary. Embrace it, nurture it, and let it guide you toward the realization of your self-belief. In the subsequent chapters, we will delve into celebrating your wins, cultivating resilience, and embracing your unique journey—each contributing to your path of self-belief and achievement

.

CHAPTER 8

CELEBRATING YOUR WINS

8.1. The Power of Celebration

Why Acknowledging Achievements is Essential for Self-Belief

In the grand symphony of life, each success, no matter how small, is a note worth celebrating. As you navigate the intricate melody of your journey, it's easy to become entangled in the pursuit of bigger goals and loftier dreams. Yet, it's equally crucial to pause, take a deep breath, and let the music of your accomplishments resonate within you. This is the essence of celebration, and it holds a profound place in the orchestra of self-belief.

The Importance of Acknowledgment

Before we explore the transformative power of celebration, let's reflect on why acknowledging achievements is essential for self-belief:

1. Fuel for Motivation: Celebrations serve as potent fuel for your motivation. When you acknowledge your successes, you ignite a fire within yourself. The memory of triumphs becomes a wellspring of inspiration, propelling you towards your next endeavor.

2. Boost to Confidence: Self-belief is intertwined with confidence. By celebrating your wins, you reinforce your belief in your abilities. Each acknowledgment becomes a building block, strengthening the foundation of your self-assurance.

3. Positive Reinforcement: Celebrations act as positive reinforcement for your efforts. They signal to your subconscious mind that your actions lead to favorable outcomes. This, in turn, encourages you to persist in your pursuits.

4. Cultivating a Growth Mindset: Celebrating your wins fosters a growth mindset. Instead of fixating on failures or shortcomings, you shift your focus towards progress and improvement. This mindset is vital for continuous self-belief.

5. Enhancing Resilience: In the face of challenges, acknowledging past successes bolsters your resilience. It reminds you that you've overcome obstacles before, and you have the capability to do so again.

The Art of Celebration

Celebration isn't merely an afterthought—it's an art that requires intention and mindfulness. Let's delve into how you can cultivate this art to enhance your self-belief:

1. Acknowledge Even the Smallest Wins: Celebrations need not be reserved for monumental achievements. Recognize and celebrate even the tiniest

victories. Did you complete a challenging task on your to-do list? Did you make progress toward a long-term goal? These are all worthy of acknowledgment.

2. Create Milestones: Break down your larger goals into milestones or checkpoints. When you reach these milestones, take a moment to celebrate your progress. It not only reinforces your self-belief but also provides an opportunity to assess and adjust your course if needed.

3. Personalized Celebrations: Celebrate in a way that resonates with you personally. Whether it's a quiet moment of reflection, a gathering with loved ones, or a special treat, choose a form of celebration that feels authentic to you.

4. Express Gratitude: Gratitude is closely tied to celebration. Take a moment to express gratitude for the effort you've invested and the progress you've made. Gratitude amplifies the positive emotions associated with your wins.

5. Document Your Achievements: Keep a record of your achievements, no matter how small. Whether through a journal, a digital document, or a vision board, having a tangible record of your successes allows you to revisit and relive them.

6. Share Your Wins: Don't hesitate to share your achievements with trusted friends, family, or mentors. Sharing your wins not only invites positive reinforcement but also strengthens your connections with those who support your journey.

Cultivating a Positive Mindset Through Celebration

Celebration is not a mere ritual; it's a mindset-shaping practice. Here's how it cultivates a positive mindset conducive to self-belief:

1. Shifts Focus to the Positive: In a world often fixated on problems and challenges, celebration redirects your focus to the positive aspects of your life. It encourages you to look for the good even in the midst of difficulties.

2. Promotes Self-Compassion: Celebration fosters self-compassion. It reminds you to treat yourself with kindness and acknowledge your efforts, just as you would celebrate a dear friend's accomplishments.

3. Strengthens Self-Efficacy: Self-efficacy, or your belief in your ability to achieve goals, is bolstered by celebration. When you repeatedly acknowledge your achievements, you reinforce your sense of competence.

4. Reduces Negative Self-Talk: Celebrations act as a counterbalance to negative self-talk. They create a reservoir of positive self-affirmation that drowns out the critical inner voice.

5. Builds a Resilient Mindset: A mindset grounded in celebration is resilient. It weathers storms with grace, knowing that even in adversity, there are lessons and opportunities for growth worth celebrating.

The Ripple Effect of Celebration

Celebration is not a solitary act. It has a ripple effect that extends far beyond your immediate experience. When you celebrate your wins, you influence others around you and contribute to a culture of positivity and self-belief:

1. Inspires Others: Your celebrations serve as an inspiration to those who witness them. They encourage others to embark on their journeys with self-belief and optimism.

2. Strengthens Relationships: Celebrating together fosters stronger bonds with friends, family, and colleagues. It creates shared moments of joy and connection.

3. Cultivates a Supportive Environment: In a community that celebrates wins, individuals feel more supported and empowered. It becomes a space where self-belief thrives.

In the grand tapestry of your life, each thread of celebration weaves a story of self-belief. It's not an act of arrogance but a testament to your journey's significance. In this chapter, we've explored why acknowledging your achievements is essential, the art of celebration, and how it cultivates a positive mindset.

As you continue your voyage, remember that celebration is your compass in the sea of self-belief. It guides you toward a brighter horizon, where the melody of your accomplishments resonates with the symphony of your dreams. In the forthcoming chapters, we'll delve into recognizing your accomplishments, cultivating resilience, and embracing your unique journey—each an integral part of your path to self-belief and fulfillment.

8.2. Recognizing Your Accomplishments

Ways to Identify and Appreciate Your Successes, No Matter How Small

In the grand tapestry of life, success is not a singular event but a mosaic of achievements, both big and small. Yet, it's all too common to overlook or downplay our accomplishments, particularly the modest ones. In this chapter, we'll embark on a journey of self-discovery, learning to recognize and appreciate our successes, regardless of their scale. This process is a vital step on the path to self-belief, as it amplifies our confidence and nurtures our self-worth.

The Pervasiveness of Modesty

Modesty, while a virtue in many contexts, can sometimes be a stumbling block on our path to self-belief. We've been conditioned to believe that boasting or acknowledging our achievements, especially the minor ones, is immodest or egotistical. This societal conditioning often leads us to overlook our successes, leaving us blind to the stepping stones of our journey.

It's crucial to recognize that recognizing your accomplishments is not an exercise in vanity. It's an act of self-compassion and self-empowerment. By acknowledging your successes, you affirm your abilities and lay the foundation for greater achievements. Let's delve into why recognizing your accomplishments is essential:

1. Boost to Confidence: When you recognize your accomplishments, you're essentially cataloging evidence of your capabilities. This boosts your confidence by reminding you of your past successes, both large and small.

2. Positive Feedback Loop: Acknowledging your achievements creates a positive feedback loop. Success breeds confidence, and confidence fuels further success. It's a self-perpetuating cycle.

3. Motivation and Momentum: Recognizing your accomplishments motivates you to pursue more goals. It creates a sense of momentum, propelling you forward on your journey.

4. Resilience: In challenging times, reflecting on your past successes can provide solace and bolster your resilience. It reminds you that you've overcome difficulties before.

5. Self-Worth: Your achievements are a reflection of your worth, your unique abilities, and your capacity for growth. Recognizing them reinforces your sense of self-worth.

The Art of Self-Recognition

Recognizing your accomplishments is an art—a practice that requires intention and mindfulness. It involves shifting your perspective, training your mind to see the value in every endeavor, and embracing a positive and appreciative attitude. Let's explore ways to cultivate this art:

1. Keep a Success Journal: Start a success journal where you document your achievements, both big and small. This can be a physical journal or a digital one. Whenever you achieve something, record it in your journal, including the date and a brief description. This practice not only helps you recognize your successes but also provides a tangible record to revisit when needed.

2. Practice Gratitude: Integrate gratitude into your daily routine. Regularly take a moment to reflect on and appreciate your accomplishments. Gratitude amplifies the positive emotions associated with success and reinforces the habit of recognition.

3. Share Your Successes: Don't hesitate to share your achievements with friends or loved ones. Sharing your successes not only invites positive reinforcement but also strengthens your connections. It's a mutually beneficial act that fosters a culture of celebration and self-belief.

4. Set Milestones: Break down your larger goals into milestones or checkpoints. When you reach these milestones, celebrate them as

achievements. This provides an opportunity to recognize your progress and adjust your course if needed.

5. Review and Reflect: Periodically, set aside time to review and reflect on your successes. This can be a weekly, monthly, or yearly practice. During these sessions, acknowledge what you've accomplished and how it has contributed to your growth.

6. Celebrate Others: Celebrating the successes of others can indirectly help you recognize your own. When you appreciate the achievements of those around you, it reinforces the value of success and encourages you to recognize your own accomplishments.

The Impact on Confidence

The act of recognizing your accomplishments has a profound impact on your confidence. It's akin to a gardener tending to a flourishing garden. As you nurture your self-belief by acknowledging your successes, your confidence blossoms. Here's how it influences your confidence:

1. Concrete Evidence: Recognizing your accomplishments provides you with concrete evidence of your abilities. It's a collection of proof that you can reference whenever self-doubt creeps in.

2. Shift in Self-Perception: It reshapes your self-perception. Instead of seeing yourself as someone who occasionally succeeds, you begin to view yourself as a capable and accomplished individual.

3. Empowerment: Recognizing your accomplishments empowers you. It instills a sense of agency, reminding you that you have control over your life and can achieve your goals.

4. Resilience: When faced with challenges or setbacks, your confidence serves as a buffer. It helps you weather the storm by reminding you of your past triumphs.

5. Courage to Dream Bigger: As your confidence grows, so does your capacity to dream bigger. You become bolder in setting goals and pursuing your aspirations, knowing that you have the ability to achieve them.

Celebrating Wins, Big and Small

Remember that recognition is not limited to grand achievements. It encompasses even the smallest of wins. In fact, celebrating minor successes is a powerful practice that trains your mind to appreciate every step of your journey. Small wins, when recognized, accumulate into substantial evidence of your capabilities.

So, celebrate the completion of a challenging task, the successful resolution of a problem, the improvement of a skill, or the consistency in pursuing your goals. Every step forward, no matter how tiny, is a step worth recognizing.

As you continue your quest for self-belief, remember that recognition is a key instrument in your toolkit. By acknowledging your accomplishments, you lay the groundwork for a confident and empowered self. This chapter has explored why recognizing your achievements is vital, the art of self-recognition, and the profound impact on your confidence.

In the forthcoming chapters, we'll delve into cultivating resilience, embracing your unique journey, and understanding the power of visualization—each a critical component of your voyage towards self-belief and fulfillment.

CHAPTER 9

THE ROLE OF RESILIENCE

9.1. Understanding Resilience as a Key Element of Self-Belief

Resilience, often defined as the ability to withstand adversity and bounce back from challenges, is not merely a quality to possess—it's a cornerstone of self-belief. In this chapter, we'll delve into the profound role that resilience plays in nurturing self-belief. We'll explore what resilience truly means, how it empowers us to confront and conquer life's trials, and why it's an indispensable element on our journey to self-belief.

The Nature of Resilience

Resilience is not a fixed trait but a dynamic process. It's the capacity to adapt positively in the face of adversity, trauma, or significant stress. Often compared to a rubber band, resilience allows us to stretch and flex without breaking, to endure hardships without losing our essence, and to spring back to our original form when the storm subsides.

Key Characteristics of Resilience:

Adaptability: Resilient individuals demonstrate a remarkable capacity to adapt to changing circumstances. They're not resistant to change but embrace it as an opportunity for growth.

Emotional Regulation: Resilience involves the ability to manage and regulate emotions effectively. This emotional intelligence enables individuals to stay composed in challenging situations.

Optimism: Resilient people tend to maintain an optimistic outlook, even in the face of adversity. They see setbacks as temporary and believe in their ability to overcome them.

Problem-Solving Skills: Resilience is closely linked to problem-solving abilities. Those with resilience can analyze challenges objectively and develop strategies to overcome them.

Social Support: Building and utilizing a support network is a hallmark of resilient individuals. They understand the value of seeking help from friends, family, or professionals when needed.

The Interplay Between Resilience and Self-Belief

Resilience and self-belief are intertwined in a symbiotic relationship. To appreciate the role of resilience in nurturing self-belief, let's explore how they complement each other:

1. Resilience Fuels Self-Belief: When you bounce back from adversity, you gain confidence in your ability to overcome challenges. Each successful resilience episode reinforces your self-belief.

2. Self-Belief Enhances Resilience: Conversely, believing in yourself provides the psychological armor needed to confront adversity with determination. It imbues you with the confidence that you can endure and emerge stronger.

3. Resilience Nurtures Positivity: Resilience equips you with the mental fortitude to maintain a positive outlook even in challenging times. This positivity, in turn, bolsters your self-belief by fostering a can-do attitude.

4. Self-Belief Fuels Persistence: When you believe in your abilities, you're more likely to persist in the face of obstacles. This persistence, a product of self-belief, is a key component of resilience.

5. Resilience Amplifies Self-Image: Overcoming adversity reinforces a positive self-image. It demonstrates your capabilities and strengthens your self-concept, vital aspects of self-belief.

6. Self-Belief Fuels Coping Strategies: Believing in yourself empowers you to employ effective coping strategies when facing adversity. This, in turn, enhances your resilience.

The Resilience-Self-Belief Feedback Loop

Imagine resilience and self-belief as two gears working in tandem, each propelling the other forward. When you face a challenge, your resilience gear engages. You adapt, persevere, and emerge stronger. This strengthens your self-belief gear, enhancing your confidence in your ability to tackle future challenges. And when the next obstacle arises, your self-belief gear kicks in, empowering you to face it with resilience.

Understanding this feedback loop is crucial because it implies that you can cultivate both resilience and self-belief simultaneously. By working on one, you inherently bolster the other. Let's delve into how you can enhance your resilience:

Strategies to Cultivate Resilience

1. Develop a Growth Mindset: Embrace challenges as opportunities for growth. A growth mindset fosters resilience by reframing setbacks as stepping stones to progress.

2. Cultivate Emotional Intelligence: Enhance your emotional regulation skills. Practice mindfulness and self-awareness to manage emotions effectively, even in stressful situations.

3. Seek Social Support: Build and nurture a support network. Don't hesitate to seek help when facing difficulties. Sharing your challenges with others can provide new perspectives and solutions.

4. Set Realistic Goals: Establish achievable goals and break them down into manageable steps. This approach prevents overwhelm and allows you to track your progress.

5. Practice Self-Compassion: Treat yourself with kindness and understanding, especially when you stumble. Self-compassion enables you to bounce back from setbacks more gracefully.

6. Develop Problem-Solving Skills: Enhance your ability to analyze problems and devise effective solutions. Problem-solving is a cornerstone of resilience.

7. Maintain a Supportive Inner Dialogue: Replace self-criticism with self-encouragement. Develop a positive inner dialogue that reinforces your belief in your capabilities.

8. Learn from Setbacks: Instead of dwelling on failures, extract lessons from them. What can you learn from past challenges that will make you more resilient in the future?

9. Practice Flexibility: Be open to change and adaptable in your approach. Rigidity can hinder resilience, as it resists the natural ebb and flow of life.

10. Maintain Physical Well-being: A healthy body supports a resilient mind. Prioritize exercise, nutrition, and adequate rest to bolster your resilience.

The Resilience of the Human Spirit

Throughout history, the human spirit has demonstrated remarkable resilience in the face of extraordinary challenges. It's a testament to the indomitable nature of the human psyche. Each tale of triumph over adversity, whether in personal narratives or on a grand societal scale, underscores the incredible power of resilience.

Understanding the role of resilience in self-belief is not just an academic exercise; it's a journey of self-discovery and personal growth. As you cultivate resilience, you empower yourself to navigate life's unpredictable terrain with confidence and conviction.

9.2. Developing Resilience

Practical Tips and Exercises for Building Resilience

In the previous section, we examined the profound role of resilience in nurturing self-belief. We understood that resilience is not an inherent trait but a dynamic process that can be cultivated and strengthened over time. Now, in this chapter, we will delve into the practical aspects of developing resilience. We will explore a range of tips, exercises, and strategies that you can incorporate into your life to enhance your ability to withstand adversity and bounce back stronger than ever.

The Importance of Developing Resilience

Why should you actively work on developing resilience? The answer lies in the benefits it offers:

Enhanced Mental Health: Resilience is closely associated with improved mental well-being. It equips you with the tools to manage stress, anxiety, and depression more effectively.

Increased Emotional Intelligence: Cultivating resilience enhances your emotional intelligence. You become better at recognizing, understanding, and regulating your own emotions, as well as empathizing with others.

Improved Problem-Solving Skills: Resilience involves adaptive problem-solving. As you develop resilience, you become more adept at finding creative solutions to challenges.

Better Coping Mechanisms: Resilient individuals possess a diverse toolkit of coping mechanisms. They are better equipped to handle stressors without resorting to unhealthy behaviors.

Greater Self-Belief: Developing resilience naturally reinforces your self-belief. Each time you overcome adversity, your confidence in your ability to handle future challenges grows.

Practical Tips for Building Resilience

1. Embrace Change and Uncertainty: Change is a constant in life. Embrace it as an opportunity for growth rather than resisting it. Accept that uncertainty is part of the human experience.

2. Cultivate a Growth Mindset: Adopt a mindset that views challenges and setbacks as opportunities for learning and development. Embrace failures as stepping stones to success.

3. Develop Emotional Regulation Skills: Practice mindfulness, meditation, or deep breathing exercises to improve emotional regulation. The ability to stay calm under pressure is a hallmark of resilience.

4. Set Realistic Goals: Establish achievable goals and break them down into smaller, manageable steps. This prevents overwhelm and allows you to track your progress.

5. Build a Support Network: Foster positive relationships with friends, family, mentors, and peers. Don't hesitate to seek their support and guidance during difficult times.

6. Practice Self-Compassion: Treat yourself with kindness and understanding, especially when you face setbacks. Avoid self-criticism and negative self-talk.

7. Develop Problem-Solving Skills: Hone your ability to analyze problems objectively and devise effective solutions. Problem-solving is a cornerstone of resilience.

8. Learn from Setbacks: Instead of dwelling on failures, extract lessons from them. Consider what you can learn from past challenges to enhance your resilience in the future.

9. Maintain a Supportive Inner Dialogue: Replace self-criticism with self-encouragement. Cultivate a positive inner dialogue that reinforces your belief in your capabilities.

10. Stay Physically Active: Regular exercise has numerous mental health benefits, including stress reduction and improved mood. Physical well-being supports resilience.

Resilience-Building Exercises

1. Journaling: Maintain a resilience journal where you document your challenges, setbacks, and your emotional responses to them. Reflect on how you can approach similar situations differently in the future.

2. Visualization: Practice visualization exercises where you imagine yourself successfully overcoming challenges. Visualization can enhance your self-belief and mental resilience.

3. Role Models: Identify individuals you admire for their resilience. Study their stories and strategies for bouncing back from adversity. Use their experiences as a source of inspiration.

4. Mindfulness Meditation: Incorporate mindfulness meditation into your daily routine. Mindfulness helps you stay present and calm in the face of stressors.

5. Stress Inoculation: Gradually expose yourself to controlled stressors to build resilience. Start with minor challenges and progressively work your way up to more significant ones.

6. Self-Care Rituals: Develop self-care rituals that prioritize your mental and emotional well-being. Whether it's a daily walk in nature, reading, or listening to soothing music, self-care is crucial for resilience.

Real-Life Stories of Resilience

Abraham Lincoln: From Failure to the Presidency

Abraham Lincoln's life was marked by numerous failures and setbacks. He failed in business, lost several elections, and experienced personal tragedies. However, Lincoln's resilience and belief in his ability to lead the nation through turbulent times never wavered. He went on to become one of America's greatest presidents, guiding the country through the Civil War and issuing the Emancipation Proclamation. Lincoln's journey exemplifies how resilience and self-belief can transform one's destiny.

Oprah Winfrey: Rising from Adversity

Oprah Winfrey faced a challenging childhood marked by poverty and abuse. Despite these early hardships, she persisted in pursuing her dreams. Oprah's resilience and unwavering belief in her potential propelled her from a local radio host to a global media mogul. Her story inspires countless individuals to overcome adversity and build resilience on their journey to self-belief.

Developing resilience is not an overnight process; it's a lifelong journey of self-discovery and growth. By incorporating practical tips, exercises, and the wisdom of real-life resilience examples, you can cultivate the mental and emotional fortitude needed to navigate life's challenges. Remember that resilience is not a solitary endeavor; seeking support from others and fostering a positive inner dialogue are essential components of your resilience toolkit. As you build resilience, you fortify the foundation of self-belief, empowering yourself to face adversity with confidence and grace.

CHAPTER 10

AVOIDING THE COMPARISON TRAP

10.1. Exploring the Dangers of Constant Comparison

In today's hyperconnected world, it's easier than ever to fall into the comparison trap. The rise of social media, coupled with a culture that often equates success with external markers such as wealth, fame, or physical appearance, has made comparison a pervasive aspect of modern life. This chapter is dedicated to understanding the perils of constant comparison and learning how to break free from its grip. We'll delve into the psychological, emotional, and even physical consequences of relentless comparison, and most importantly, we'll explore strategies to cultivate self-acceptance and self-love.

The Age of Comparison

We live in an era where we are constantly bombarded with curated images of people's lives. Social media platforms display meticulously filtered snapshots of seemingly perfect moments. These platforms, while providing a valuable means of connection and expression, can also be breeding grounds for comparison.

The comparison trap is a psychological phenomenon where individuals assess their worth by measuring themselves against others. It often involves scrutinizing others' achievements, possessions, appearance, and even happiness, and drawing conclusions about our own lives based on these comparisons.

The Dangers of Constant Comparison

1. Undermined Self-Esteem: One of the most evident consequences of constant comparison is a decline in self-esteem. When you constantly measure yourself against others and find yourself lacking, your self-worth diminishes.

2. Jealousy and Envy: Comparison often leads to feelings of jealousy and envy. Instead of celebrating others' success, you may find yourself resenting it. These emotions can be toxic to your well-being and relationships.

3. Anxiety and Depression: The pressure to meet unrealistic standards set by comparisons can lead to anxiety and depression. It's emotionally taxing to constantly worry about measuring up.

4. Inauthentic Living: When you base your choices and actions on what you believe will garner approval or validation from others, you compromise your authenticity. This can result in a life that feels hollow and unfulfilling.

5. Stagnation: Constant comparison can paralyze you with fear of failure. You might avoid taking risks or pursuing your passions because you fear not measuring up to the achievements of others.

6. Physical Health Implications: The stress and negative emotions stemming from comparison can have physical health implications, such as elevated blood pressure and compromised immune function.

Breaking Free from the Comparison Trap

1. Practice Mindfulness: Mindfulness involves being fully present in the moment and non-judgmentally accepting your thoughts and feelings. When you're mindful, you're less likely to engage in negative self-comparisons.

2. Limit Social Media: While social media has its benefits, it's crucial to consume it mindfully. Set boundaries on your social media use, unfollow accounts that trigger negative comparisons, and curate your feed to include content that inspires and uplifts you.

3. Focus on Intrinsic Values: Shift your focus from extrinsic markers of success to intrinsic values. Instead of seeking external validation, reflect on what truly matters to you and what brings you joy and fulfillment.

4. Practice Gratitude: Regularly express gratitude for the positive aspects of your life. Gratitude can counteract feelings of envy and help you appreciate what you have.

5. Set Personal Goals: Establish goals and benchmarks that are meaningful to you personally, rather than aiming to match someone else's achievements. Strive for growth and progress, not perfection.

6. Cultivate Self-Compassion: Treat yourself with the same kindness and understanding that you would offer a friend. Remember that everyone has their struggles and insecurities.

Cultivating Self-Acceptance and Self-Love

1. Self-Acceptance: Self-acceptance involves embracing yourself, flaws and all. It's an acknowledgment that you are a unique individual with your own

set of strengths and weaknesses. Self-acceptance is the foundation upon which self-love is built.

2. Self-Love: Self-love goes beyond self-esteem. It is an active practice of caring for your physical, emotional, and mental well-being. It involves treating yourself with kindness, prioritizing self-care, and nurturing a positive self-image.

3. Affirmations: Positive affirmations are statements you can repeat to reinforce self-love and self-acceptance. For example, "I am worthy of love and respect," or "I embrace my uniqueness."

4. Self-Compassion: Self-compassion is treating yourself with the same compassion you would offer to a friend in times of struggle or suffering. It involves self-kindness, recognizing your common humanity (that we all make mistakes), and mindfulness.

5. Seek Support: Sometimes, building self-acceptance and self-love may require the guidance of a therapist or counselor. Don't hesitate to seek professional help if you find yourself struggling with these aspects.

The Liberating Journey of Self-Acceptance

The journey to self-acceptance and self-love is not linear or without its challenges. It's a path of self-discovery, reflection, and growth. It's about letting go of the need for external validation and embracing the uniqueness that makes you who you are. It's a journey that liberates you from the confines of constant comparison and allows you to live authentically and wholeheartedly.

Remember that your worth is not determined by how you measure up to others. You are inherently valuable just as you are. Embracing your unique journey means celebrating your individuality, flaws, and imperfections. It's about recognizing that your worth is not contingent on external factors but is an intrinsic part of your being.

The dangers of constant comparison are real and pervasive in today's world, but they are not insurmountable. By understanding the psychological impact of comparison and actively working to break free from its grip, you can pave the way for a healthier, more authentic, and fulfilling life. Embracing your unique journey, practicing self-acceptance, and cultivating self-love are transformative steps toward living a life that is truly your own, untethered by the need for constant validation from external sources.

10.2. Staying True to Yourself

Embracing Your Individuality and Uniqueness

In a world that often celebrates conformity and uniformity, staying true to yourself is a radical act of self-affirmation. This chapter explores the profound significance of embracing your individuality and uniqueness. We will delve into the concept of authenticity, the societal pressures that can erode it, and the transformational power of self-acceptance in cultivating unwavering self-belief.

The Call for Authenticity

Authenticity is a term frequently used today, but what does it truly mean? At its core, authenticity is about being true to yourself, your values, and your beliefs. It's the art of living in alignment with your innermost essence rather than conforming to external expectations.

The Pressure to Conform

From an early age, we are exposed to societal norms and expectations. These norms dictate how we should look, behave, and even think. The desire for acceptance and belonging often compels us to conform, even if it means suppressing our true selves.

The Costs of Conformity

While conformity can provide a sense of belonging, it often comes at a significant cost. When you suppress your authentic self to fit into a mold created by others, you may experience:

Emotional Dissonance: The conflict between your true feelings and the emotions you express to conform can lead to emotional dissonance.

Loss of Identity: Over time, conforming to external expectations can erode your sense of identity, leaving you feeling disconnected from your true self.

Diminished Self-Esteem: Continuously conforming to others' standards can lead to a decline in self-esteem as you perceive your authentic self as inadequate or unacceptable.

Stagnation: Conformity can hinder personal growth and development by discouraging you from exploring your unique potential.

The Beauty of Individuality

Embracing Uniqueness

Your individuality is what sets you apart from everyone else on the planet. It encompasses your distinctive experiences, perspectives, talents, and quirks. Embracing your uniqueness is an act of self-love and self-acceptance.

The Authenticity Paradox

Paradoxically, the more you embrace your individuality and authenticity, the more likely you are to attract like-minded individuals who appreciate you for who you truly are. Authenticity has a magnetic quality that draws people to you.

How Self-Acceptance Contributes to Unwavering Self-Belief

Self-acceptance is the cornerstone of self-belief. It's the unwavering acknowledgment that you are worthy of love, respect, and success just as you are. Here's how self-acceptance fuels unwavering self-belief:

1. Inner Harmony: When you accept yourself fully, you align your inner beliefs with your actions and aspirations. This inner harmony breeds self-belief because there is no internal conflict undermining your confidence.

2. Resilience: Self-acceptance acts as a shield against external criticism and judgment. You are less affected by others' opinions when you deeply accept yourself, which bolsters your resilience.

3. Authentic Confidence: The confidence that stems from self-acceptance is authentic and unshakeable. It doesn't rely on external validation or accomplishments but on a profound sense of self-worth.

4. Risk-Taking: Self-acceptance empowers you to take risks and pursue your passions without the fear of failure or judgment. This willingness to take chances is often a catalyst for success.

5. Healthy Boundaries: Self-acceptance enables you to set healthy boundaries in relationships and situations. You are more likely to say no when necessary and protect your well-being.

Practical Steps to Embrace Your Individuality and Cultivate Self-Acceptance

1. Self-Reflection: Take time for self-reflection. Explore your values, passions, and the aspects of your true self that you may have neglected or hidden.

2. Self-Compassion: Practice self-compassion by treating yourself with the same kindness and understanding that you would offer a dear friend.

3. Mindfulness: Embrace mindfulness to stay connected with your thoughts and emotions. Mindfulness allows you to observe self-criticism without judgment.

4. Embrace Imperfection: Understand that perfection is an unattainable ideal. Embrace your imperfections as unique qualities that make you who you are.

5. Set Authentic Goals: Align your goals with your authentic self, not with societal expectations. Pursue aspirations that genuinely resonate with you.

6. Surround Yourself with Acceptance: Seek out supportive relationships that accept and celebrate your true self. Limit time spent with those who undermine your authenticity.

7. Celebrate Small Wins: Acknowledge and celebrate even small steps toward self-acceptance and embracing your individuality. Each step forward is a victory.

The Empowering Journey of Self-Discovery

Staying true to yourself and embracing your individuality is a transformative journey. It's about rediscovering and nurturing the person you were born to be, free from the constraints of societal expectations. It's a journey that leads to self-acceptance, which, in turn, fuels unwavering self-belief.

Remember that embracing your individuality doesn't mean rejecting personal growth or change. It's an invitation to evolve authentically, guided by your values and inner compass. It's a journey of self-discovery that empowers you to live a life that is uniquely and unapologetically your own.

The path to staying true to yourself is both liberating and empowering. It's an affirmation of your worthiness and an embrace of your uniqueness. As you cultivate self-acceptance and align your life with your authentic self, you'll discover that unwavering self-belief naturally follows. This belief in yourself is a profound force that propels you toward your goals and allows you to navigate life's challenges with resilience and grace. So, embark on this journey with an open heart, for it leads to a life lived on your terms, where your individuality is celebrated, and your self-belief knows no bounds.

EMBARKING ON YOUR SELF-BELIEF JOURNEY

As we reach the final chapter of this transformative journey towards self-belief, I want to extend my heartfelt congratulations to you. You've shown dedication and determination in exploring the depths of self-belief, and you've acquired valuable insights and practical strategies to begin your personal odyssey towards unwavering self-confidence.

Your Self-Belief Journey Begins Now

You are standing at the threshold of a remarkable journey, one that has the potential to reshape your life, your aspirations, and your relationship with yourself. The pages you've turned, the words you've read, and the insights you've gained are not mere intellectual exercises; they are the seeds of transformation.

Belief in oneself is not a destination; it's a continuous expedition. It's a journey of self-discovery, growth, and empowerment that unfolds each day as you navigate life's ebbs and flows. Your self-belief journey is about nurturing the unshakable confidence that resides within you.

The Power of Taking Action

At this juncture, I encourage you to take the first step on this path, for it is in action that your belief in yourself finds its truest expression. You've equipped yourself with the knowledge and tools needed to embark on this expedition, and now it's time to put them into practice.

Remember that belief without action is like a compass without a map; it may point you in the right direction, but it won't take you there. It's your actions that will solidify your self-belief, refine your character, and mold your destiny. So, what's your first step? What action can you take today to align yourself with your aspirations?

Setting Meaningful Goals

Perhaps your initial action involves setting meaningful goals that resonate with your core values and desires. Use the wisdom you've gained in earlier chapters to create SMART (Specific, Measurable, Achievable, Relevant, Time-bound) goals. These goals will be the milestones along your self-belief journey, signposts marking your progress.

Embracing Your Uniqueness

Or maybe your journey commences with a deep embrace of your uniqueness. Understanding that you are one-of-a-kind, with a blend of talents, quirks, and experiences that no one else possesses, is a cornerstone of self-belief. Embrace your individuality as your greatest strength, for it is what sets you apart in this vast world.

Overcoming Self-Doubt

For some, the first step might involve recognizing and challenging self-doubt. Recall the strategies you've uncovered in Chapter 3, and use them to confront that persistent inner critic. Replace self-doubt with self-assuredness, and watch your confidence soar.

Fostering Resilience

Others may decide to cultivate resilience, as discussed in Chapter 9. Resilience is the armor that shields your self-belief during the inevitable storms of life. By practicing resilience, you'll not only weather challenges but emerge from them stronger and more self-assured.

Building a Supportive Network

For some, the journey could entail building a supportive network, as emphasized in Chapter 5. Surround yourself with friends, mentors, and allies who uplift you, celebrate your victories, and bolster your self-belief. Remember that the company you keep significantly influences your mindset.

The Role of Visualization

Visualization, as discussed in Chapter 6, can be your starting point. Craft vivid mental images of your future success, and allow these visions to infuse you with self-belief. Visualization is not a passive act; it's a dynamic tool that can propel you forward.

Taking Action

Finally, for many, the most crucial initial step is taking action, highlighted in Chapter 7. Belief fuels action, and action reinforces belief. It's a symbiotic relationship. Choose a goal, no matter how modest, and take that first step today. The momentum you build will carry you farther than you can imagine.

Final Words

As we wrap up this journey, I wish to share some final words of inspiration and motivation. Consider these as the fuel that will power your self-belief engine:

"Within you lies an unquenchable wellspring of potential. Your self-belief is the key to unlock it. Trust in your abilities, your resilience, and your unique journey. Remember that every great achievement began with a single belief – the belief that it was possible. As you venture forward, know that I believe in you, your potential, and your capacity to create the life you desire. Your journey towards unwavering self-belief has begun, and with each step, you'll find yourself closer to your dreams." - Positive B. White

Your journey towards self-belief is an ongoing narrative, a tapestry woven with the threads of your experiences, aspirations, and growth. As you traverse this path, take solace in the knowledge that self-belief is not a finite resource; it's a boundless wellspring within you. It replenishes with each challenge you conquer, each goal you achieve, and each obstacle you surmount.

In Closing

With these final words, I encourage you to take that first step towards your self-belief journey. The path may be winding, and the terrain may change, but always hold onto the unwavering conviction that you are capable of greatness.

The world is filled with individuals who once stood where you are now, individuals who chose self-belief over doubt, action over stagnation, and resilience over resignation. They are living proof that this journey leads to remarkable destinations.

As you embark on this journey, may your self-belief grow stronger with each passing day. Embrace your uniqueness, set your goals, overcome self-doubt, and celebrate your wins. Cultivate resilience, surround yourself with positivity, and visualize your success. Most importantly, take action. Your journey towards unwavering self-belief has begun, and with each step, you'll find yourself closer to your dreams.

Thank you for taking this voyage with me. May your belief in yourself illuminate your path and empower you to reach new heights. You have everything you need within you. Believe it. Live it. Achieve it.

Made in the USA
Columbia, SC
04 December 2024

48381700R00067